Beautiful Paper Stars

Beautiful Paper Stars
Craft Decorations for Every Season

Ursula Stiller, Armin Täubner
and Gudrun Thiele

Floris Books

Translated by Anna Cardwell
Models by Ursula Stiller, Armin Täubner and Gudrun Thiele
Photography: Frechverlag GmbH
Hand drawn illustrations: Atelier Schwab

First published in German as *Das Große Sternbuch*
by Frechverlag GmbH in 2012
First published in English by Floris Books in 2015

© 2012 Frechverlag GmbH, Stuttgart
English version © Floris Books 2015

This edition is published by arrangement with
Claudia Böhme Rights & Literary Agency, Hanover
(www.agency-boehme.com)

British Library CIP data available
ISBN 978-178250-207-4
Printed in China through Asia Pacific Offset Ltd

Contents

Before You Begin

This book is divided into six different star types: Aurelio, Filino, Froebel, Messina, Solino and Venezia. Each section begins with the basics for that particular star type and its variations, followed by some exciting project ideas and tips for decorating your home.

Difficulty level

Once you grasp the basics for each star type, you can build your confidence as you progress. Projects are ordered from beginner to expert within each section.

★ Beginner

★★ Intermediate

★★★ Expert

Essential materials

At the start of each project, you'll be told which materials are unique to that project. In almost every case, however, you will also need the following:

◊ Pencil
◊ Eraser
◊ Scissors
◊ Ruler
◊ Multi-purpose glue or thin double-sided tape
◊ Clothes pegs (clothespins)
◊ String to hang the star
◊ Craft knife
◊ Cutting mat

Additional tools to make life easier

◊ Bone folder
◊ Empty ballpoint pen
◊ Nail file
◊ Needle and thread
◊ Matches
◊ Paper pricking tool
◊ Hole punch
◊ Stapler

Choosing your paper

Exact folding is the key to a successful star. The paper you choose should be easy to fold and quite stiff. A smooth surface allows the segments to be tucked into each other and glued together.

The golden rule for star making is: the smaller the star, the thinner the paper. For larger stars you should use heavier paper. Very large stars with a paper size of over 30 x 30 cm (12 x 12 in) will need paper up to 150 gsm (100 lb) to remain stable. A bone folder (typically made from plastic rather than bone nowadays!) is very useful for folding paper heavier than 90 gsm (60 lb).

Tracing and tissue paper are not suitable, but thicker types of translucent paper or lantern paper are strong enough to hold their shape. Remember, however, that when many layers of translucent paper overlap they may lose their glow!

Aurelio Stars

Aurelio stars: the basics

Paper

Origami paper is best for these stars as the segments are made from perfect squares. Paper should ideally be between 90 and 120 gsm (60 and 80 lb), depending on the size of the star.

How to fold Aurelio star segments

1. Fold the paper square in half lengthways and open out again. Then fold all four corners in to meet at the centre point.

2. Turn the square over and make sure the fold line is vertical. Fold the right side up to the centre fold to make a narrow point at the bottom. Fold the left side down to the centre fold to make a narrow point at the top. Always begin folding the right side first, as segments where the left side is folded first will not slot together later.

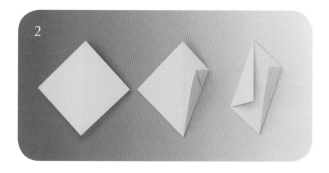

3. Turn the paper over. Fold the right and left corners in to meet the centre fold, making a diamond shape. This side will be the inside of the star and will not be visible later. The small top right and the bottom left triangles are gluing flaps.

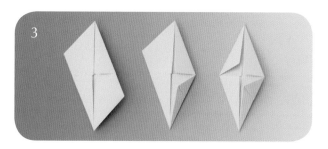

4. Turn the diamond over, fold in half and unfold again. This side will be the outside of the star. There should be a small diagonal pocket at the top right of the diamond, and another at the bottom left.

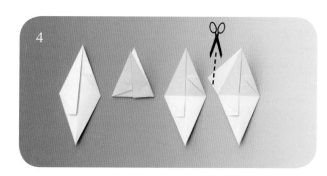

> **Tip**
> It helps to snip the corners of the underside flaps to aid their slotting in.

Joining star segments

To attach each new piece, unfold the top left flap at the back of the new segment, apply glue to its underside and tuck it into the top right pocket of the first segment.

Gluing segments out of stronger paper

Segments folded out of stronger paper will need gluing in some places to keep them together. Fold the segments as before, but glue the loose triangles in Step 2 down.

After finishing the stars, glue the pockets shut too. To do this, apply glue to the front edge of a cardboard strip, insert the strip into the pocket, press the pocket gently shut, pull the cardboard strip out and press together firmly.

> **Tip**
> Use pegs or paperclips to hold down the flaps while the glue sets, or use a glue roller so there is no drying time.

Gluing the segments together

It is important to tuck the glued flap into a pocket quickly, as the glue may become overly sticky. If you cannot tuck the flap completely into the pocket for this reason, remove it and let both segments dry. Stop the pocket sticking to itself by inserting the tip of a nail file and rotating it.

Once both segments are dry again, apply some fresh glue and repeat the attempt swiftly.

> **Tip**
> For a very smooth finish, we recommend using a solvent-based adhesive.

Hanging up the stars

Tie your desired string halfway along a matchstick, then push the matchstick into a gap between segments. It should flatten against the paper and hold the model firmly.

Flat Aurelio star

1. Take twelve pink 15 x 15 cm (6 x 6 in) and twelve purple 10 x 10 cm (4 x 4 in) pieces of paper and fold into diamond segments as described on page 10. Make two six-pointed stars out of the larger pink segments as shown.

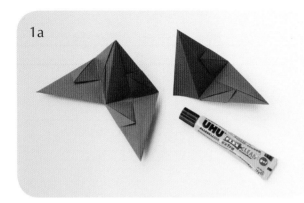

2. Glue the purple segments on top of the points of the pink stars for decoration.

3. Turn the stars over. Glue the flaps on the back and secure with pegs as shown.

4. Offset the two six-pointed stars with their backs to one another as shown. Before gluing, secure with pegs. Then, removing two pegs at a time, fold each point upwards, apply glue, and secure again with pegs.

5. Alternatively, you can glue the two stars with their points aligned to make a six-pointed star.

Five-pointed stars

For five points instead of six, make ten Aurelio diamond segments and follow the instructions above, but with one less segment per flat star.

Small Aurelio star

1. Fold eight segments as described on page 10.
2. Join two segments as described on page 10. Add two more segments and squeeze inwards to complete a four-pointed star. Repeat steps 2a and 2b to make another four-pointed star.

3. Glue both stars back to back with their flat points aligned. With some practice you can fold the flaps of one segment around the point of the second, insert and glue it into the pocket.

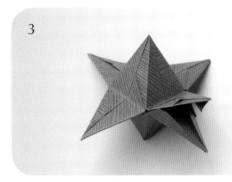

4. Alternatively, you can offset the stars to make an eight-pointed star. Once correctly placed, secure with pegs and glue point by point as described on page 12, step 4.

3D Aurelio star

1. You will need twelve folded segments.
2. Glue the first two segments together as described on page 10. The third segment however should slot into the second segment's lower left pocket as shown, rather than its upper right pocket.

3. Attach the fourth segment in the same way as the third, then complete the ring by slotting the flap of the first segment into the pocket of the fourth segment.

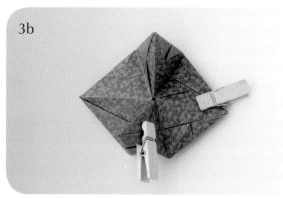

4. Fold to make a four-pointed star.

5. Slot and glue a new segment into the top right pocket. Add three segments to the other sides in the same way, so that the shape resembles a windmill.

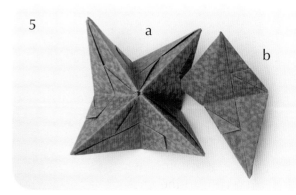

6. For each of the original points, there should be an outer flap remaining (a). Lift this flap, fold over the new outer segment and tuck into its nearest pocket (b). This makes a solid, 3D point. Then secure the remaining three points in the same way, and turn over.

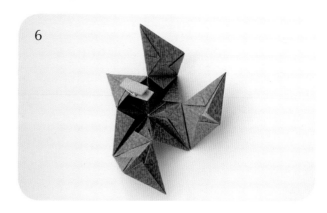

7. Glue a new segment to the top right point as shown. Repeat for the other three sides.

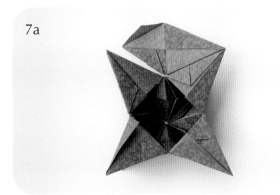

7a

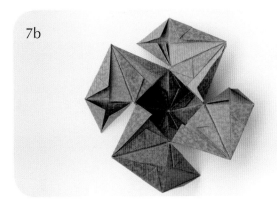

7b

9. Remove the pegs, fold the four sides in towards the centre and secure into four points.

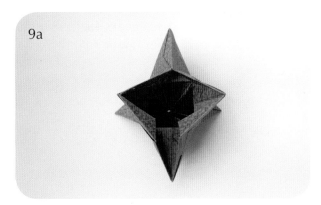

9a

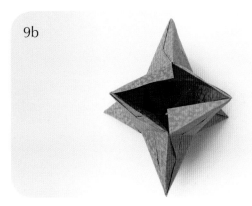

9b

8. Secure the remaining unattached flap of each inner segment to the new segments. First move each flap over the top of its new adjacent segment, then glue into its top pocket and hold in place with a peg as shown. Repeat for the other three segments.

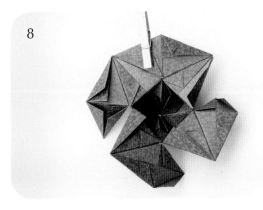

8

Large Aurelio star

As these stars get larger, they get more complex. To keep things clear, this model is divided into different colours for different stages. In this case, five segments constitute each stage so you will need thirty in total.

First stage: yellow

1. Open a yellow gluing flap, apply glue and insert into the pocket of the second segment.

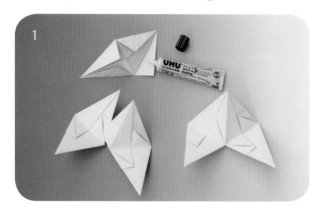

2. Insert the third segment to the lower pocket between the other two points, as in the 3D Aurelio star on page 13.

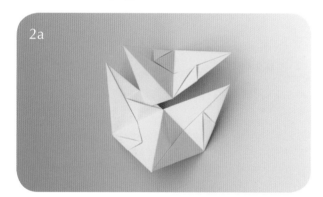

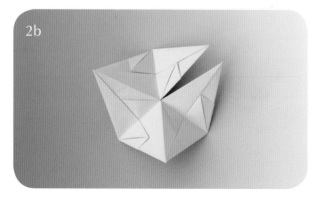

3. Add a fourth segment to the third segment.

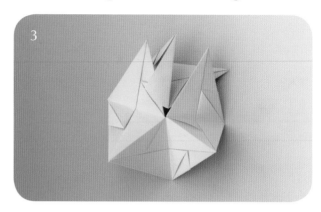

4. Finally, add a fifth segment and attach at both ends to complete a five-pointed rosette – the first stage is complete.

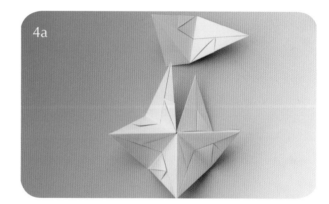

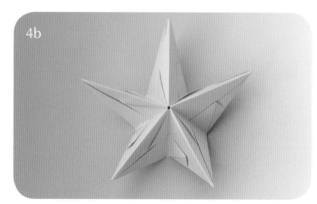

16

Second stage: orange

1. Open an orange gluing flap, apply glue to the back of it and insert into the outside pocket of a yellow segment.

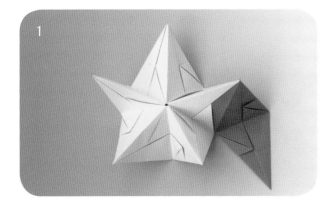

2. Attach a second segment in the same way.

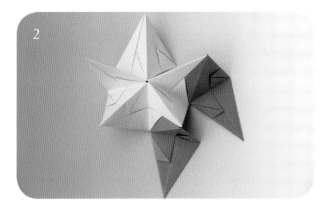

3. Do the same with the remaining three segments to form a windmill shape.

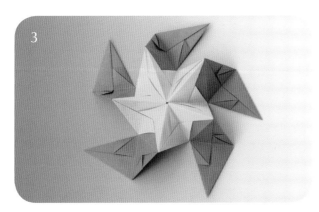

4. Turn this windmill shape over.

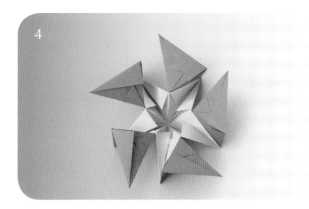

5. Open a yellow flap from the first stage and apply glue. Fold it over the orange segment adjacent to it and insert the yellow flap into its pocket to make a sturdy point. Repeat this process with the remaining four points.

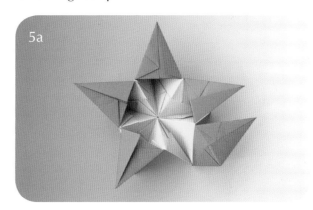

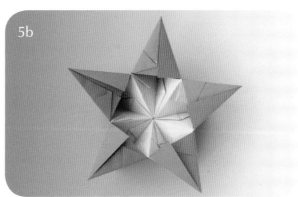

Turn over for more instructions ▶▶

6. This is what the front should look like.

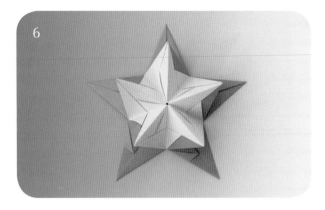

Third stage: red

1. Open up the gluing flap of a new red segment. Attach it to the pocket of an orange (second stage) segment.

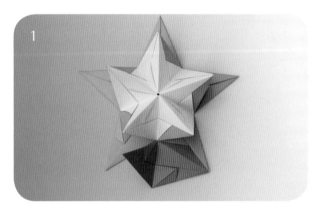

2. Add four further red segments in the same way.

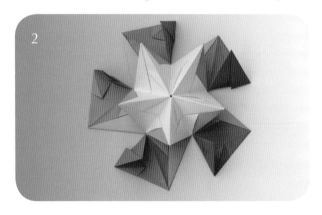

3. This is how the shape should look on the back. Turn over again to continue gluing.

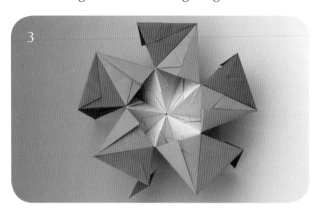

Fourth stage: red again

1. Glue the flap of a new red segment into the pocket of one of the red segments from the third stage as shown.

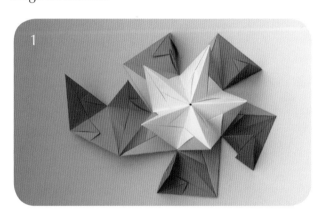

2. Turn the star over and bring these two red segments around until they meet an orange segment from the second stage. Insert the flap of the orange segment into the pocket of the red segment and glue in place. This makes a 3D triangular point.

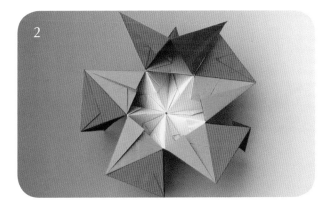

3. Repeat steps 1 and 2 for the remaining four points. The star should now have ten 3D points.

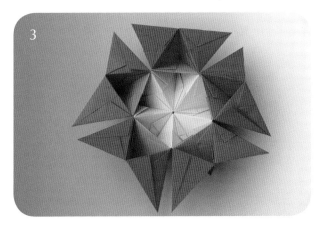

4. Attach two red triangles from adjacent points together.

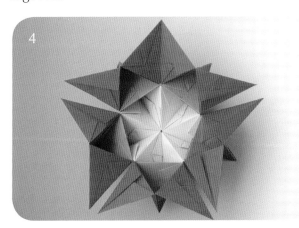

5. Repeat this process around the star as shown.

Fifth stage: orange again

1. Glue a flap of a new orange segment into the pocket of a red segment from stage four.

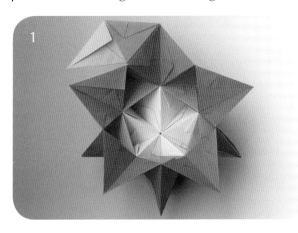

2. Attach the remaining four orange segments in the same way.

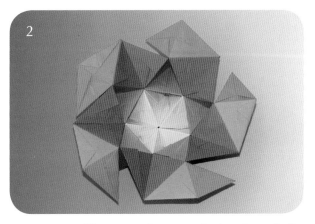

Turn over for more instructions ▶▶

3. Fold the orange segment (shown at the top of the photo) over the wide point made from two red segments and attach to make a new, 3D triangular point.

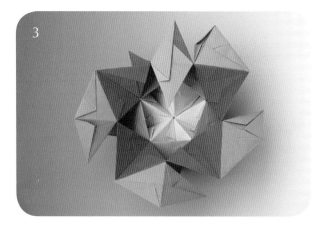

4. Repeat this process with the remaining four orange segments. Now your star will have fifteen points.

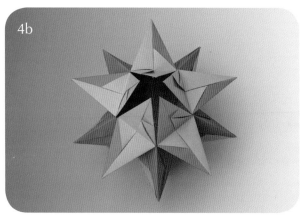

Sixth stage: yellow again

1. Glue the flap of a new yellow segment into an orange pocket from the fifth stage.

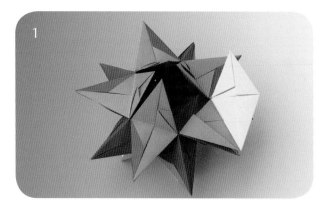

2. Attach the remaining segments in the same way.

3. Glue an orange flap from the fifth stage into the pocket of an adjacent yellow segment. Repeat for the other four points. Now at the top of the star you should have a star-shaped hole.

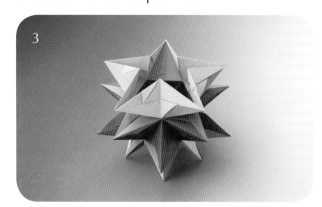

4. Open up all the remaining flaps of the yellow segments.

5. Insert the flaps into the pockets of their neighbouring yellow segments. Make sure all flaps point out as you work: once the gap is closed you will not be able to reach inside! Before gluing the last segments together, insert a matchstick with string attached.

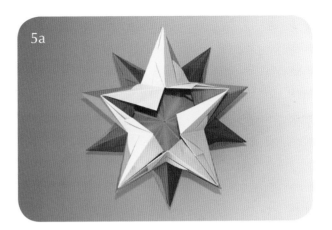

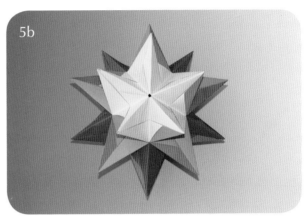

Pink and purple decorations

Brighten up your workspace

Star size: 16–22 cm
(6–9 in)

You will need

Pink and purple star (top left)

◊ 20 sheets of purple origami paper,
10 x 10 cm (4 x 4 in)
◊ 10 sheets of pink origami paper, 10 x 10 cm
(4 x 4 in)

Large decorated star (top right)

◊ 30 sheets of lilac origami paper, 20 x 20 cm
(8 x 8 in)
◊ Scraps of pink card for decorative shapes

Small decorated star (bottom right)

◊ 10 sheets of pink origami paper, 10 x 10 cm
(4 x 4 in)
◊ Scraps of silver paper or star stickers for
decoration

Pink star with pink diamonds (middle left)

◊ 8 sheets of dark pink origami paper,
15 x 15 cm (6 x 6 in)
◊ 8 sheets of light pink origami paper,
10 x 10 cm (4 x 4 in)

Lilac and purple star (bottom left)

◊ 6 sheets of purple origami paper,
10 x 10 cm (4 x 4 in)
◊ 6 sheets of lilac origami paper, 10 x 10 cm
(4 x 4 in)

Large decorated star

For an entirely lilac star, follow the instructions for the large Aurelio star on pages 15–21 with lilac paper at every stage.

Then cut out sixty stars from scrap paper and glue one on each side of each point.

Small decorated star

Make two five-pointed stars following the instructions on page 12. Align the stars back to back and glue the points to each other.

Decorate liberally with star stickers or cut-outs of your own design.

Pink star with pink diamonds

Make two four-pointed stars from dark pink paper following the instructions on page 13. Fold segments out of the light pink paper and glue them to the centre of the points. Offset the points and glue both stars back to back.

Lilac and purple star

Make two six-pointed stars following the instructions for the flat Aurelio star on page 12. Alternate the colour for each section. Offset the points and glue both stars back to back.

Pink and purple star

Follow the instructions for the large Aurelio star on pages 16–21. Use purple segments for stages one and two, use pink segments for stages three and four, and use purple segments again for stages five and six.

Red and white lights

Make your own lamp

Star size: 45 cm (18 in)

Luminous red star

You will need

Luminous red star

◊ 30 sheets of red lantern paper, 30 x 30 cm
  (12 x 12 in)
◊ Lamp fixture or fairy lights
◊ Photo adhesive

Luminous red and white star

◊ 30 sheets of red lantern paper, 30 x 30 cm
  (12 x 12 in)
◊ 30 sheets of white lantern paper,
  17 x 17 cm
◊ Decorative stars
◊ Lamp fixture or fairy lights
◊ Photo adhesive

1. For either star, fold thirty sheets of red lantern paper into Aurelio segments using the basic instructions on page 10.
2. Then follow the instructions for the large Aurelio star on pages 16–21, leaving the final two segments unglued – this will provide a space for the light fixture later.
3. For the red and white star, fold thirty more white Aurelio segments and glue them in place inside each point.
4. Stick or glue on some decorative stars.
5. Insert the lamp fixture or fairy light into the gap you left earlier. Carefully glue the final sections into place so that the cable holds firmly.

Golden red suns

Warm and bright

Star size: 10–35 cm (4–14 in)

You will need

Orange star (top left)
◊ 30 sheets of orange patterned paper, 20 x 20 cm (8 x 8 in)

Yellow star (bottom left)
◊ 30 sheets of yellow textured paper, 15 x 15 cm (6 x 6 in)

Red star with orange decorations (centre right)
◊ 12 sheets of red paper, 20 x 20 cm (8 x 8 in)
◊ Scrap orange paper

Red star with five or ten points (centre left; centre)
◊ 10 sheets of thick red patterned card, 15 x 15 cm (6 x 6 in)

Red star with six points (bottom centre)
◊ 6 sheets of red textured paper, 10 x 10 cm (4 x 4 in)

Miniature red star with gold decorations (top right)
◊ 8 sheets of red paper, 5 x 5 cm (2 x 2 in)
◊ 16 gold stars

Tip
You can always make coloured origami paper more interesting by gluing stars to it.

Orange star and yellow star

Make the stars following the instructions for the large Aurelio star on pages 16–21, see also 'gluing segments out of stronger paper' on page 11.

Red star with orange decorations

Following the instructions for the 3D Aurelio star on pages 14–15. Glue the pockets shut. Cut out twenty-four decorative stars and glue them on.

Red star with five or ten points

Make two five-pointed stars each following the instructions for the flat Aurelio star with five points on page 12.

For five points, align the stars back to back and glue together. Or you can offset the points so that the star has ten points.

Red star with six points

With red textured paper, follow the instructions for a small Aurelio star on page 13, using only three segments per star, rather than four. Offsetting the two stars will create six points altogether.

Miniature red star with gold decorations

Make two stars with four segments each following the instructions for the small Aurelio star on page 13. Offset the points and glue together, then decorate with gold stars.

Classic variations

Shiny and traditional

Star size: 18–23 cm (7–9 in)

· ·

You will need

Large gold star (top centre; bottom right)

◊ 30 sheets of gold shiny or matte textured paper, 15 x 15 cm (6 x 6 in)

Six-pointed star (bottom left; centre; top right)

◊ 12 sheets of gold textured paper, 15 x 15 cm (6 x 6 in) or 7.5 x 7.5 cm (3 x 3 in)

◊ Scraps of gold textured paper or star stickers

White and gold star

◊ 6 sheets of white origami paper, 10 x 10 cm (4 x 4 in)

◊ 6 sheets of gold origami paper 10 x 10 cm (4 x 4 in)

◊ Star stickers or other decorations

· ·

Large gold star

Follow the instructions for the large Aurelio star on pages 16–21. You may also want to revisit the tips for gluing segments out of stronger paper on page 11.

Six-pointed star

Make two six-pointed stars by following the flat Aurelio star instructions on page 12. Glue both stars back to back with the points aligned.

If you would like to decorate it further, apply stickers or cut out and glue on star shapes.

White and gold star

Make two six-pointed stars following the instructions for the flat Aurelio star on page 12. Alternate the colours for each segment. Glue both stars back to back with the points aligned.

Twinkling stars

Personalise your fairy lights

Star size: 11 cm (4 ½ in)

You will need

Per star
◊ 30 sheets of white lantern paper, 8.5 x 8.5 cm (3 ½ x 3 ½ in)
◊ Photo adhesive
◊ Fairy lights

1. Make as many stars as you need by following the instructions for the large Aurelio star on pages 16–21. In this case, when you get to the end of each star, leave a segment unglued so that you can insert a fairy light.

2. Insert a fairy light into the gap, then seal the final segment over the top.

3. Make sure that the cable is held at the centre of a rosette.

Filino Stars

Filino stars: the basics

Paper

As with the Aurelio star, paper between 90 and 120 gsm (60 and 80 lb) is best for Filino stars.

Making and tracing around the templates

1. Photocopy the template and increase to the desired size.
2. Glue onto sturdy card to make a reusable template.
3. Cut out carefully, using a craft knife and cutting mat.
4. Place the template on your desired coloured paper and trace around the edges with a pencil. Then cut along the lines with a craft knife.
5. You may want to cut some short slits (1 – 2 mm) into the segments at the edges of the dashed lines to ease folding. These places are marked with small arrows in the template section on pages 146–149.

Hanging up the stars

Attach your hanging string to a small wooden bead. Place the end with the bead into the star just before the last segment is glued in place.

> ### Tip
> Use opaque coloured paper or card for making these stars as the insides will be visible through their cut-out patterns.

Lantern paper

Transparent or translucent paper can be glued to the interior of segments. It should be cut to fit just inside the frame.

Eight-pointed Filino star

1. Turn to page 146 for the 'Stars within stars' template. For this practice run, you need not cut out the interior pattern – simply use the template to provide the general shape of the star so you can see how it fits together.
2. Transfer the photocopied template to your desired paper as described above, and produce eight versions – which we will call 'segments'.
3. On each template, you will see tabs marked A, B and C. Eight-pointed stars require four segments with three tabs and four segments with two tabs. Therefore, on four of your segments, you will need to remove tab C.
4. Make tiny cuts (1 – 2 mm) at the small black arrows, then fold the segment along its dashed lines. Glue the segment together using either double-sided tape or all-purpose glue. (Double-sided tape will not work with very intricate stars). The black triangle symbol marks the tip of this finished segment. Repeat until you have completed eight segments: four with three tabs and four with two tabs.

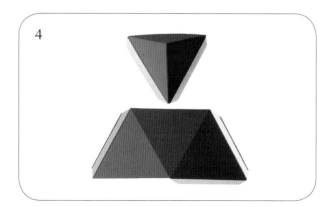

5. Start with the segments which originally had three tabs. Glue the segments to each other anticlockwise. With segment 1 on the right, glue segment 2's tab to segment 1 as shown. The edge of segment 2 without a tab should be at the bottom.

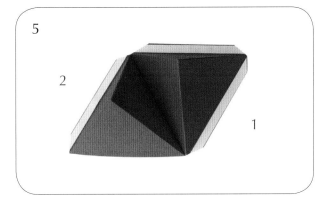

6. Attach segment 3 to segment 2 in the same way. The edge without a tab should now be at a diagonal angle to the right of the point.

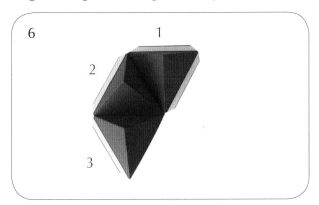

7. Glue segment 4 in place. The edge without a tab is at a diagonal angle to the right of the point

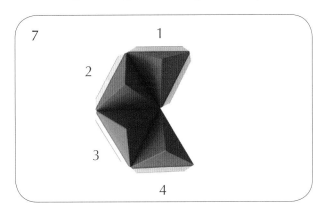

8. Fold inwards and attach segment 4 to segment 1.

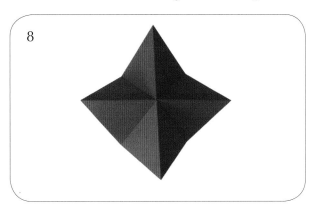

9. Turn the four-pointed section over. The thin white lines in the photo are the tabs.

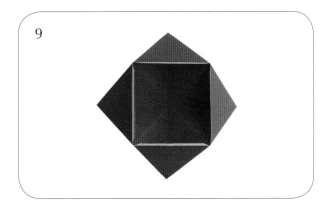

10. Now use the remaining four segments which originally had only two tabs. Attach segments 5–8 to the tabs on segments 1–4 as shown. All remaining tabs should be pointing in the same direction.

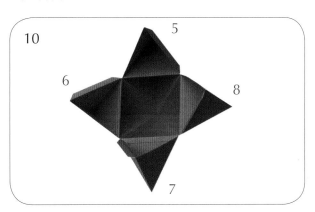

Turn over for more instructions ▶ ▶

11. Join segments 5 and 6.

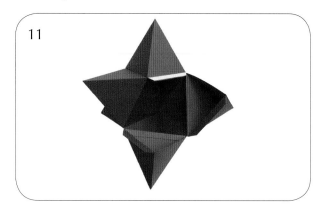

12. Join segments 6 and 7.

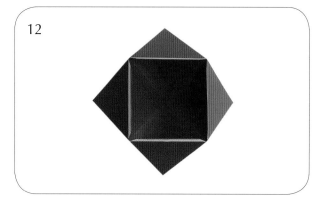

13. Join segments 8 and 5. Use all-purpose glue for this as you cannot reach inside to press the edges together. Alternatively, glue the last two tabs to the outside of the points.

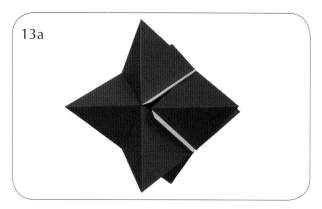

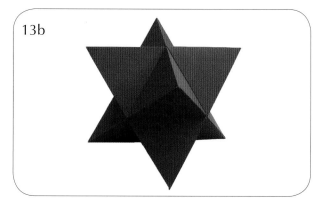

Tip

Very fine stars can be glued using all-purpose glue as their tabs are less than 6 mm (¼ in) wide and will not be large enough for double-sided tape. You can always insert tweezers into the cut out holes of very fine stars to press the glued edges together.

Twenty-pointed Filino star

1. Use the 'Christmas trees' template on page 148, but again ignore the interior cut-out design so you can simply build the shape.
2. Cut out, score and fold ten segments with three tabs and ten segments with two tabs (remove the c tabs).

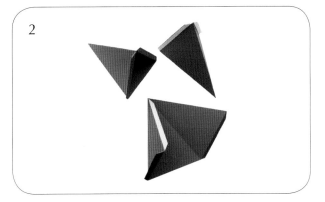

Tip
You may want to number the segments as you practise, so you can keep an eye on them.

---

3. First, glue the segments with three tabs. Glue segment 2 to segment 1 in an anticlockwise direction, with segment 1 on the right hand side. Segment 2's edge without a tab should be at the bottom.

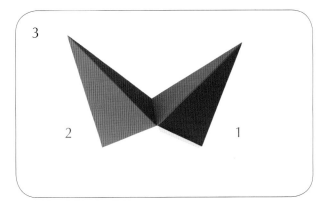

4. Now join segments 3–5.

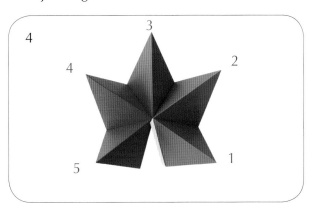

5. Join points 5 and 1. This makes a five-pointed star. Turn the five-pointed star over.

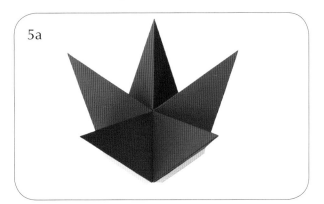

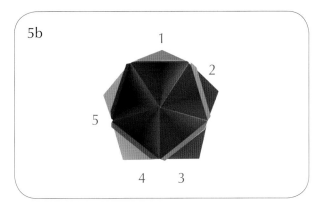

Turn over for more instructions ▶▶

6. Now attach five more three-tab segments. Join segment 6's edge without a tab to point 1's remaining tab.

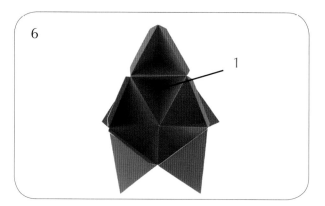

7. Attach segments 7–10 anticlockwise as shown.

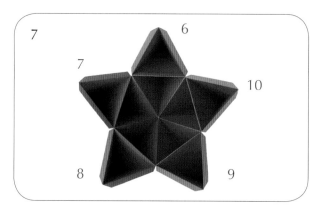

8. Now attach five of the segments which originally had only two tabs. Join segment 11 so the edge without a tab is facing to the left.

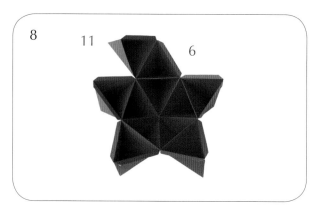

9. Now glue segments 12–15 in the same way.

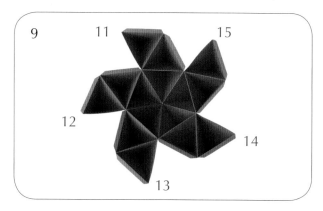

10. Join adjacent segments 11 and 7. Here you can see the white double-sided tape of segment 11's tab.

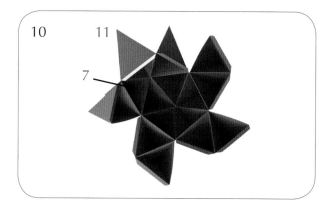

11. Join segments 12 and 8 in the same way.

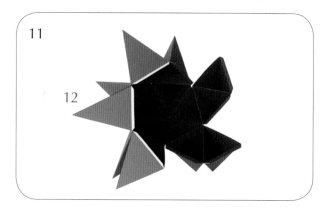

12. Repeat for segments 13 and 9, 14 and 10, and 15 and 11.

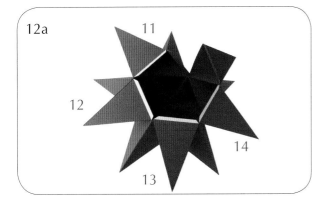

12a

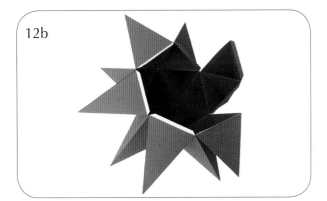

12b

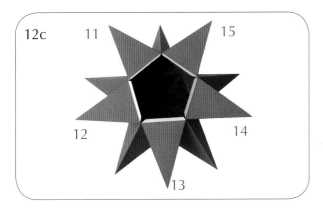

12c

13. Now attach the final few segments. To do this, glue segments 16–20 to segments 11–15 with their tabs facing anticlockwise as shown.

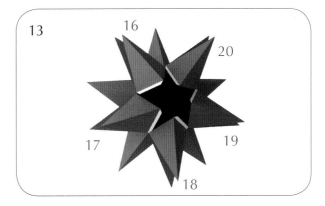

13

14. Now join segment 20 to segment 16.

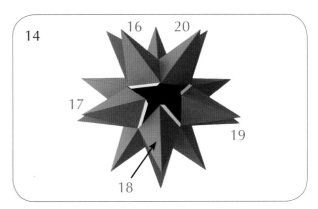

14

15. Repeat for segments 16 and 17, then 17 and 18, then join segment 19 to 18 and 20. Use all-purpose glue as you will not be able to reach inside the star. Alternatively you can glue these last two tabs to the outside of the point.

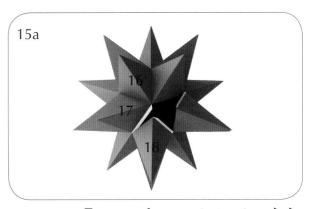

15a

Turn over for more instructions ▶▶

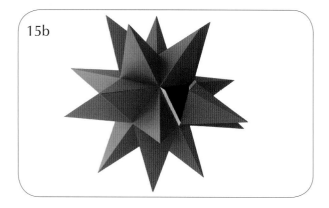

15b

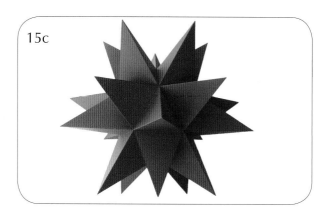

15c

Filino sphere

1. To make the sphere, use the 'Three suns' template on page 147, but again ignore the interior cutout design. Build twelve five-sided segments. You will need six segments with three tabs and six segments with two tabs (remove the C tabs in this case as always).

2. The positioning of the tabs is important for this model. Use the image below or the diagram on page 147 to lay down six three-tab segments as demonstrated.

2

3. Glue the five outer segments to the centre segment.

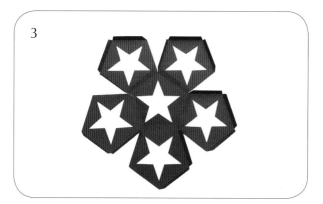

3

4. Join the outer segments to their adjacent segments one by one.

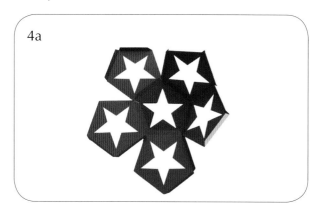

4a

4b

6b

5. Next, attach five of the remaining two-tab segments as shown.

5

7. Glue the final segment in place, and if desired, insert some string attached to a wooden bead before sealing closed.

7a

6. Now fold inwards and join these segments to their adjacent segments.

6a

7b

Stars within stars

In serene blue colours

Star size: 20 cm (8 in)

. . . .

You will need

◊ Strong paper with a blue or silver sheen,
  3 x A4 (US letter)
◊ Pale blue lantern paper, 3 x A4 (US letter)

. . . .

Template

◊ See page 146

Produce eight segments with cut-out star patterns from the template suggested.

Glue lantern paper on the underside of each segment so that light will gently glow through the design.

Then follow the instructions for the eight-pointed Filino star on pages 34–36. You will not be able to use double-sided tape as the tabs are too thin, so use all-purpose glue throughout.

Star sphere
Strong but delicate

Star size: 14 cm (5 ½ in)

You will need

◊ Gold textured card, 3 x A4 (US letter)

Template

◊ See page 146

Using the template provided, follow the instructions for the Filino sphere on pages 40–41. The tabs of this ornamental sphere are very narrow so you will need to use all-purpose glue.

Tip
This star will look particularly beautiful with translucent paper in a complementary colour behind the cut-out design. You can make a variety of star spheres in this way by varying the interior colours.

Three suns

Placed together in shining glory

Star size: 15 cm (6 in)

· ·
·
· You will need
·
· ◊ Copper or gold textured paper, 3 x A4
·   (US letter)
· ◊ White or orange lantern paper, 3 x A4
·   (US letter)
·
· ·

Template

◊ See page 147

Transfer your chosen template to create twelve segments. Once the segments are cut, glue some lantern paper behind each design. Then assemble each globe following the instructions for the Filino sphere on pages 40–41.

Ladder star

In bold red

Star size: 38 cm (15 in)
Pendant length: 15 cm (6 in)

You will need

Star
◊ Sturdy red card, 10 x A4 (US letter)

Pendant
◊ Sturdy dark blue card, A5 (US half letter)
◊ Lantern or mulberry paper, white or yellow, A5 (US half letter)

Template

◊ See page 148

Tip
Glue the last two tabs to the outside of the point if it is lined with lantern paper as you will not be able to reach inside to press the tabs together.

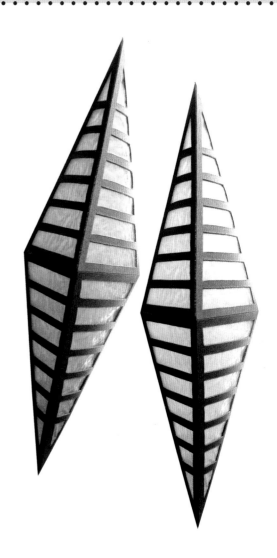

Star

Cut out twenty striped segments from the template, then follow the instructions for the twenty-pointed Filino star on pages 37–40. Use all-purpose glue for this star as double-sided tape won't fit on the delicate tabs.

Pendant

The alternate pendant template can be used to make a stunning icicle shape. Cut out your complete segment and glue lantern or mulberry paper (if desired) to the back.

As you fold inwards and construct the shape, make sure to glue the tabs to the corresponding side with the same letter.

To hang the pendant, tie a bead to one end of a thread and place in the point before gluing together.

Christmas trees

Fir tree designs

Star size: 38 cm (15 in)

You will need

◊ White or red textured card, 10 x A4
   (US letter)
◊ Optional white lantern paper, 10 x A4
   (US letter)

Template

◊ See page 148

Make this winter white star following the instructions for the twenty-pointed Filino star on pages 37–40. Use glue instead of double-sided tape as the tabs are too narrow.

Alternatively, for a more Christmassy feel, use red card and add white lantern paper on the interior.

Steeple star

Spectacularly spiky

Star size: 30 cm (12 in)

You will need

◊ Thick gold card, 10 x A4 (US letter)

Template

◊ See page 149

Make this graceful star following the instructions for the twenty-pointed Filino star on pages 37–40. As the tabs are very narrow you will not be able to use double-sided tape.

Love hearts

For Valentine's day

Star size: 30 cm (12 in)

Pendant length: 14 cm (6 in)

You will need

Star
◊ Thick red card, 10 x A4 (US letter)

Pendant
◊ Thick, dark blue card, A5 (US half letter)
◊ Mulberry or lantern paper, white or blue, A5 (US half letter)

Template

◊ See page 149

Star

Follow the instructions for the twenty-pointed Filino star on pages 37–40. Use all-purpose glue as the tabs may be too narrow for double-sided tape.

Pendant

Use the alternate template to make a pendant, then glue lantern paper to the back of the design.

Next, glue each tab to its corresponding letter as you fold the segment together.

Hang the pendant with a bead and thread before sealing the final tabs, as described on page 34.

Froebel Stars

Froebel stars: the basics

Paper

Paper of roughly 110 gsm (75 lb) should be used for making Froebel stars.

Hanging up the stars

To hang up the stars diagonally, it is easiest to attach the thread to the small gap between the three flat points at a corner.

Simple Froebel star with four strips

1. Fold two strips of paper in half and hang one over the other at a 90° angle (a). Then hang a third strip over the second strip in the same way (b). Next, hang a fourth strip over the third strip and weave it inside the first strip (c).

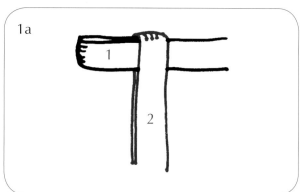

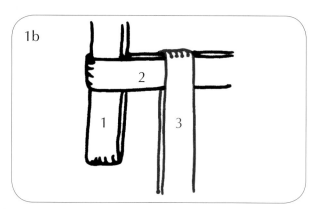

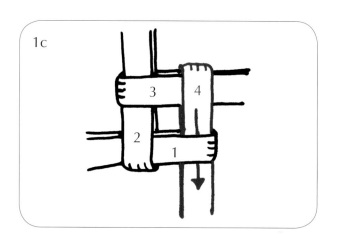

2. Carefully pull the strips until they fit snugly together.

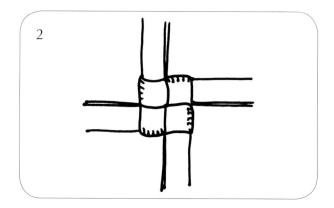

3. Turn the woven work over. Then, using the uppermost strips only: fold from bottom to top (a); from left to right (b); from top to bottom (c); and finally from right to left, threading this final strip through the loop created by the first strip (d). Pull to fit snugly again (e).

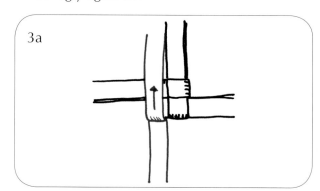

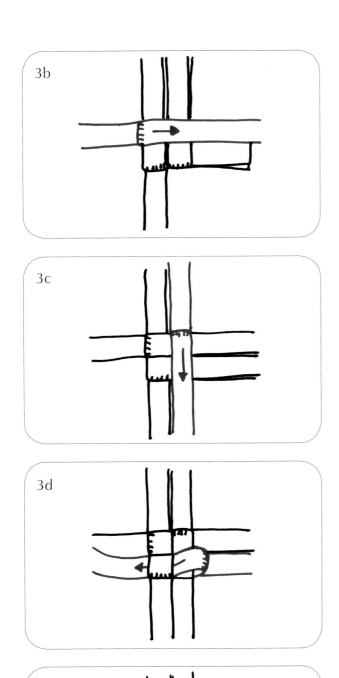

4. To make the side points, fold one strip back diagonally to the side as shown (a). Then turn this strip downwards and fold over the front again, before folding the left half **b** on top of half **a** (b) and tucking it into the top left square (c). It's easier to do this if you hold the point back slightly. Make the other three points in the same way, turn over and repeat on the other side. This makes a flat star without 3D points (d).

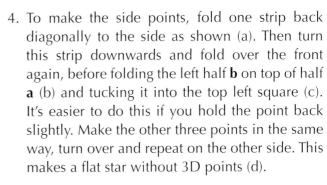

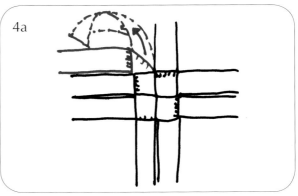

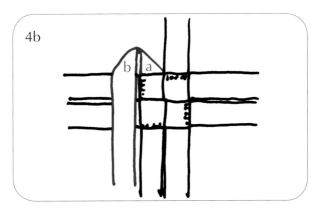

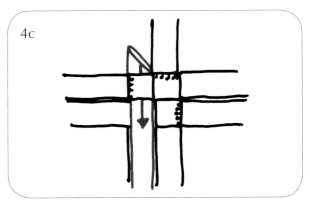

Turn over for more instructions ▶ ▶

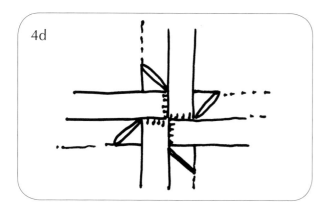

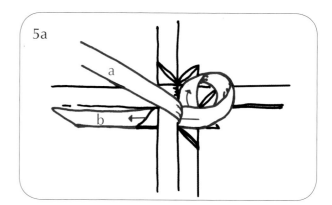

5. Finally, make the 3D points. Move strip **a** out of the way, curl strip **b**, which is pointing upwards, back as shown and weave it under **a** (a). The strip will need to be trimmed close to the flat points. Repeat with the other three points by turning the star 90° clockwise each time (b). Turn the star over and repeat for the underside.

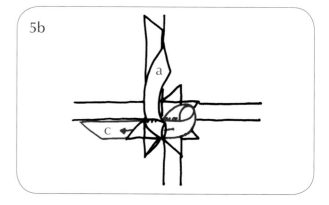

Complex Froebel star with twelve strips

1. Start with steps 1a–1c for the simple Froebel star. Extend the first strip by pulling the folded edge out a little, and then add the fifth and sixth strips as shown. Pull all the strips to fit snugly. Repeat these steps with the remaining six strips.

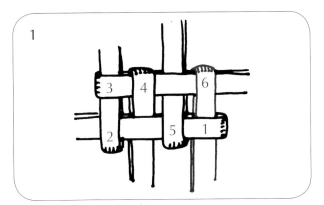

2. Connect the two sections together: move the top strips **1** and **2** out of the way (a), then tuck the bottom strip **1** into **b** and the bottom strip **2** into **a** (b). Now tuck the bottom strip **3** into **d** and the bottom strip **4** into **c** (b). Fold the figure after each set of four squares to make a cube (c).

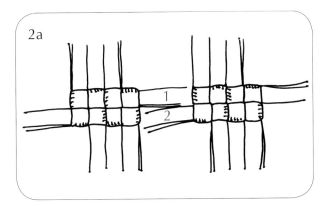

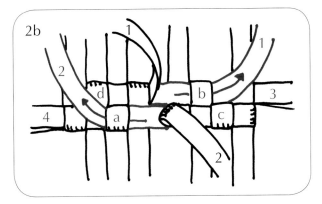

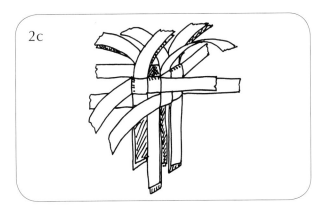

3. To complete the cube, fold the following: **a** to the right; **b** over **a**; **c** over **b**; **d** over **c** and under **a**.

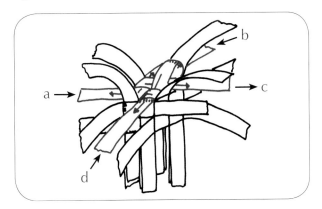

4. To make the flat points, follow steps 4a to 4c of the simple Froebel star and repeat on all six sides.
5. Make the 3D points following steps 5a to 5b of the simple Froebel star. It is easiest to complete one side before starting the next. Trim the completed ends as you work.

Christmas decorations

With added tassels

You will need

◊ Red paper, A2 (16.5 x 23.5 in)
◊ Decorative beads and gems in red, orange, pink and pearl
◊ Red cotton thread
◊ Scrap paper

Tip
A star decoration makes a lovely Advent gift.

Simple decoration

1. Fold the paper in half lengthways and cut four strips per star, each strip 2.5 cm (1 in) wide. Follow the instructions for the simple Froebel star on pages 56–58 and then decorate as desired or as shown with beads and gems.
2. To make some decorative tassels, wind your red cotton thread around a strip of scrap paper. Slide the paper out, tie one end of the bundle securely and cut the other end open. Then trim all the loose ends to one length.
3. Attach some beads to the hanging thread, pull the thread through the star with a long needle, thread some more beads at the other end and tie a loop for hanging on your tree!

Complex decoration

1. Fold the paper in half lengthways and cut twelve strips per star, each 1.5 cm ($^5/_8$ in) wide. Make a complex Froebel star following the instructions on page 59 and adorn with beads and gems.
2. Make a tassel as described above in step 2.
3. Add some beads to the hanging thread and pull through the star as described above in step 3.

Star cards

And decorative clips

Card height: 14.8 cm (5 ¾ in)

Clip size: 8 cm (3 ⅛ in)

You will need

Per clip

- ◊ 4 strips of white, red or brown patterned paper, 1.5 cm (⅝ in) wide
- ◊ Gold or pearl gems, diameter 6 cm (¼ in)
- ◊ Wooden pegs
- ◊ Gold marker pen

Per card

- ◊ White or cream card, A6 (quarter US letter)
- ◊ Extra decorative patterned paper
- ◊ Brown glitter and glitter glue
- ◊ Gold marker pen

Clips

Make a simple Froebel star by following the instructions on pages 56–58, but only making 3D points on one side. Decorate the star with beads or gold marker pen and glue to the peg.

Cards

1. To make the card on the left of the picture, cut four 1.5 cm (⅝ in) wide strips and follow the instructions for the simple Froebel star on pages 56–58, but leave out the 3D points. Glue the remaining long strips on the bottom of the star to the card as shown, then decorate as desired.

2. To make the card on the right, fold a flat star without points as above. Glue three separate vertical strips to the card and position as shown. Glue a 3 x 3 cm (1 ¼ x 1 ¼ in) square in the centre of the star for a neat central pattern, then decorate as desired.

3. To make the card at the bottom of the picture, make two flat stars out of 1.5 cm (⅝ in) and 2 cm (¾ in) wide strips respectively. Place two 1.5 cm (⅝ in) strips and one 2 cm (¾ in) wide strip vertically on the card and glue everything in place as shown.

Flowering garland

Perfect for spring

Garland length: 55 cm (22 in)

You will need

◊ Translucent flowery patterned paper,
   50 x 61 cm (20 x 24 ¼ in)
◊ 12 pink beads
◊ Pink cotton thread

Tip

It might help to glue the strips in place before trimming them, as translucent paper can be slippery.

---

1. This decorative piece consists of five simple Froebel stars, which can be made using the instructions on pages 56–58. For the larger star (top left), cut four 2.5 cm (1 in) wide strips. For the four smaller stars, cut sixteen 2 cm (¾ in) wide strips.

2. Knot the cotton thread at one end and attach some beads before using it to hang the stars. To stop the stars from slipping on the thread, you can add stopper beads at each end: do this by threading the cotton through the bead twice. You can now move the bead along the thread without it slipping.

Gift-wrapping stars

For beautiful presents

Large star size: 13 cm (5 1/8 in)
Small star size: 10 cm (4 in)

You will need

Large star

◊ 4 strips of pink paper, 1.5 cm (5/8 in) wide
◊ 8 strips of patterned translucent paper,
 1.5 cm (5/8 in) wide, 11 cm (4 1/4 in) long
◊ 2 red beads or gems

Small star

◊ 4 strips of patterned translucent paper,
 1.5 cm (5/8 in) wide
◊ 4 pink strips, 1.5 cm (5/8 in) wide, 11 cm
 (4 1/4 in) long
◊ 2 red beads or gems

Large star

1. Follow the instructions on pages 56–58 to fold a simple Froebel star out of pink paper, trimming the ends after it has taken shape. Glue a decorative bead to the centre of each side.
2. Glue the first patterned strip into the top left point, bring it round and glue it to the adjacent point on the right. Twist the strip in the same way that you would to make a 3D point.
3. Repeat for the other three sides, then turn the star over and do the same for the underneath.

Tip
When you glue the top strips, remember to leave the underneath free so that you can do the same on the other side!

Small star

1. Follow the instructions on pages 56–58 to make a simple Froebel star with the patterned paper strips. Trim the ends and glue a bead to the centre of each side.
2. Take the first pink strip and glue it into the top right flat point. Bring it over and glue it into the bottom left point.
3. Rotate the star and glue the second strip in the same way. Then turn the star over and invert the steps from earlier, that is, start at the top left and end at the bottom right.

Festive wreath

To hang on your door

Wreath size: 18 cm (7 in)

You will need

◊ 60 gold, 60 red and 12 strips of metallic red paper, each 1 cm ($^3/_8$ in) wide
◊ Red decorative beads
◊ Malleable wire, 50 cm (20 in) long
◊ Red sewing thread
◊ Pliers

1. Follow the instructions for the complex Froebel star on pages 58–59 to make five gold stars, five red stars and one metallic red star.
2. Now wind your wire around a round object to shape it into a circle, then bend one end into a small loop. Thread the stars diagonally onto the wire, alternating red and gold. Push the other end of the wire through the small loop and bend back to close the wreath.
3. Double-thread a long needle and knot the end. First add a bead to the top, then thread the needle through the red metallic star to hang it in the centre of the wreath.
4. To finish it off, add some holly leaves and hang on your door!

Supernova

Exploding red and silver

You will need

◊ Silver corrugated cardboard, A2 (17 x 24 in)
◊ 28 red and 24 strips of silver paper, each 1.5 cm ($^5/_8$ in) wide
◊ 26 red beads
◊ Tracing paper
◊ Scrap card
◊ Red sewing thread

Template

◊ See page 150

1. To make your large star, trace the template, glue to card and cut out. Place the template onto the corrugated cardboard, outline and cut out. Repeat this so that you have two corrugated stars, then glue them back to back.
2. Now start folding your simple Froebel stars using the instructions on pages 56–58. Make seven stars out of red strips and six out of silver strips.
3. Glue a red bead to the centre of each star. Then affix these stars around the large star as shown. To finish, hang one final small star in the centre and suspend the completed piece.

Poinsettias

A Christmas flower

You will need

- ◊ Red and green card, A4 (US letter)
- ◊ 4 red strips of paper, 1.5 cm ($^5/_8$ in) wide
- ◊ Gold beads
- ◊ Tracing paper
- ◊ Scrap card
- ◊ Pencils: lead, dark red and green

Template

- ◊ See page 150

1. To make the centre of the flower, fold a simple Froebel star using the instructions on pages 56 – 58 but only fold one side of the star. Glue a gold bead to the centre and fold each of the flat points upwards as shown.
2. Now for the larger petals and leaves. Trace the template, glue it to some scrap card and cut it out. Place the template onto your red or green card, outline and cut out. Repeat for as many red petals and green leaves as you desire.
3. To add some detail, draw patterns in green on the red petals and red on the green leaves. Then glue the petals and leaves under the Froebel star – first the smaller, then the larger ones.

Coiled stars

Every star is unique

You will need

◊ Translucent paper, green with border
  pattern, 50 x 61 cm (20 x 24 in)
◊ Gold beads or imitation pearls
◊ Gold coloured wire

1. To make these decorations you will need to follow the instructions on pages 56 –59 to make one complex and five simple Froebel stars.
2. Make the complex star from twelve strips 1.5 cm (⁵⁄₈ in) wide.
3. For each simple star, use four strips either 2 cm (¾ in) or 1.5 cm (⁵⁄₈ in) wide.
4. Glue the beads to the stars as shown and wind wire artistically around them. Conceal the wire ends inside the stars for a professional finish.

A star is born

In its very own nebula

Star size: 15.5 cm (6 in)

. . . .

You will need

◊ Orange patterned paper, A2 (16 x 20 in)
◊ Red patterned paper, A4 (US letter)
◊ Clothes pegs
◊ Yellow cotton thread

. . . .

Outer star

1. Cut the orange paper into twenty 2.5 cm (1 in) wide strips. Make five simple Froebel stars with 3D points on one side only, using the instructions on pages 56–58. Glue the strips to the flat side and trim the ends.
2. Glue four of these stars in a row using clothes pegs to hold them together. Once dry, fashion the stars into a circle and glue. When this is dry too, glue the remaining star on one side to make a half sphere.

Inner star

1. Cut the red paper into twelve 1.2 cm (½ in) wide strips. Make a complex Froebel star following the instructions on page 59.
2. Tie a knot at one end of the thread, secure it to the inner star and then thread it through the top of the outer star so that it dangles in the middle.

Star mobile

A spectacular constellation

Mobile size: 50 cm (20 in)

You will need

◊ Silver paper, A1 (25 x 35 in)
◊ Blue patterned paper, A2 (17 x 22 in)
◊ Large and small red beads or imitation pearls
◊ Blue thread
◊ Hole punch

Large silver star

1. To make the large silver star, cut eight strips 5 cm (2 in) wide and 70 cm (27 ½ in) long.
2. Glue these back to back to make four sturdier strips, then follow the instructions on pages 56 – 58 to fold a large simple Froebel star.

Medium blue stars

1. Using the blue paper, cut sixteen strips 2.5 cm (1 in) wide.
2. Fold four simple Froebel stars with 3D points on both sides as above.

Silver and blue stars

1. Using silver paper, cut eight strips 2 cm (¾ in) wide.
2. Fold two simple Froebel stars without 3D points from these strips.
3. Then cut sixteen 1 cm (³/₈ in) strips of blue paper and fold four simple stars with 3D points on one side only.
4. Glue the blue half-stars to the silver flat stars.

Construction

Decorate all your finished stars with beads as desired. Cascade the completed stars as shown in the photo.

Star globe

Stars in orbit

Star size: 15 cm (6 in)

• •

You will need

◊ 2 sheets of red patterned paper, 50 x 61 cm (20 x 24 in)
◊ Red beads
◊ Red cotton thread
◊ Clothes pegs

• •

Red sphere

1. Cut forty 2 cm (¾ in) wide strips out of the paper and fold ten simple Froebel stars following the instructions on pages 56–58.

2. First, slot the points into one another and glue six stars in a row, securing with pegs as you go. Then glue two sets of star pairs in the same way. Once dry, shape the row of six stars into a circle and add both pairs of stars into the gaps to form a complete sphere.

3. Place a bead on to the cotton thread, double the thread and push it through one of the stars to hang the globe.

Art Deco mobile

In black and white

Mobile size: 28 cm (11 in)

- You will need

  ◊ Black and white paper, each A2
    (17 x 22 in)
  ◊ Black and white cotton thread
  ◊ Hole punch

Large simple star

1. For the large two-coloured star, cut four 3 cm (1 ¼ in) strips: two black and two white.
2. Follow the instructions for a simple Froebel star on pages 56 – 58, alternating the strips in black and white.

Smaller complex stars

1. Cut twenty-four 1 cm (³/₈ in) black strips and twenty-four white.
2. Follow the instructions for the complex Froebel star on page 59 to make four single-coloured stars.
3. Attach the finished stars to each other as shown in the photo and hang up the mobile.

Messina Stars

Messina stars: the basics

Paper

You will need slightly thicker paper for Messina stars, ideally between 150 and 180 gsm (100 and 120 lb).

Open Messina star

1. Cut a 6 mm (¼ in) wide strip of card. This is your guide strip so you can fold all the segments exactly the same. Set it flush with the top edge of a large square piece of paper.

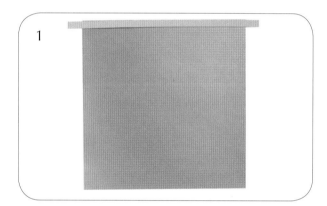

2. Fold the lower edge of the paper up to meet the bottom of the guide strip.

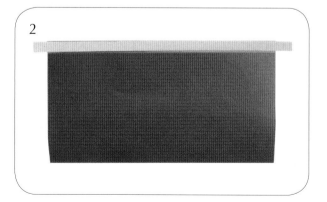

3. Remove the guide strip.

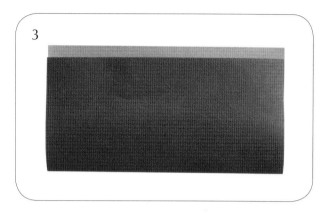

4. Before folding down the top flap, score a firm line along the top of the folded up edge with an empty ballpoint pen or bone folder. This will enable a neat fold.

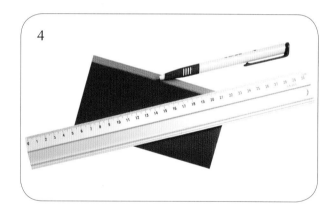

5. Apply glue to the top flap and fold down to stick over the bottom flap.

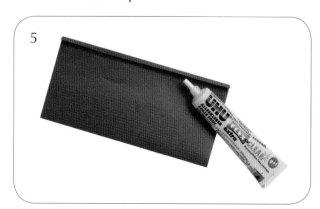

6. Balance the segment on one of the two fold lines and press down until the top fold lies exactly over the bottom fold. Flatten the sides to make two more fold lines at each side.

7. Open up to make a square tube.

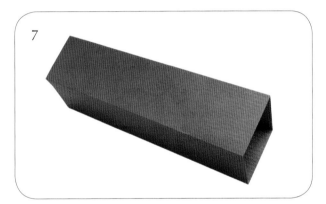

8. Collapse the two sides inwards to the centre and gently push the top surface down to create two inner fold lines.

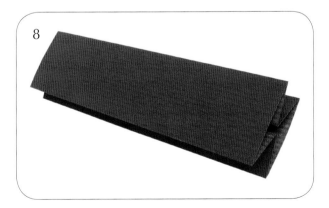

9. Position your chosen template so that it is flush with the segment edges and outline with a pencil.

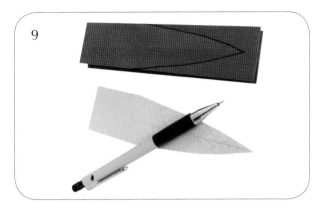

10. Cut out the point. This completes the first segment! Repeat steps 1–10 for as many segments as required for each star.

11. To glue the segments together, apply a line (or lines) of glue where the template is marked in grey. Position the second segment exactly over the first, press down and smooth.

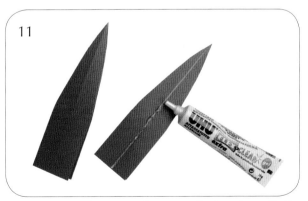

Turn over for more instructions ▶▶

12. Glue several segments to each other to make the star – this example has fourteen points. To stabilise the star, apply extra glue to the inner part of the segments, where they will all meet.

13. Unfold the star and glue the end point to the start point.

. . . .

Messina star with thread

If you use paper larger than 15 x 15 cm (6 x 6 in) or strong paper you will need to stabilise the centre by threading cotton through it.

1. Cut out the segment, then mark two holes in each segment using the template (a). Punch the holes using a hole punch (b).

2. Glue the segments together as described on pages 87–88, steps 11–13 (this example has twelve), then thread 30 cm (12 in) of cotton thread though both rows of holes. Knot the ends loosely together, leaving a fingertip's gap between knot and star to allow the star to unfold.

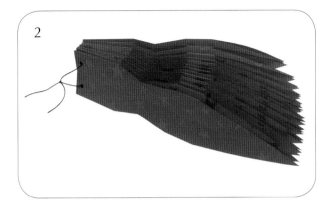

3. Unfold the star and glue the last point to the first point as before.

Closed Messina star

1. There are two templates for each closed Messina star: one start/end segment and one middle segment. Begin with the middle segments: place three or four folded segments exactly over each other and secure the photocopied template on top with several paper clips.

2. Cut out the segments with a craft knife and ruler.

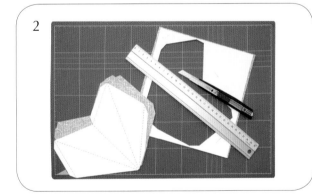

3. Place the template beside the segments and, using the template as a guide, score the folding lines using a ruler and empty ballpoint pen or bone folder. The template shows dashed lines (valley folds) and dot-dashed lines (mountain folds): score and then fold the dashed lines first; then turn the paper over before scoring the dot-dash line(s) and folding.

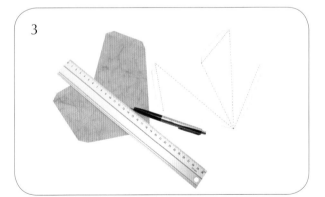

Tip
An empty ballpoint pen is ideal for scoring as the small rotating ball will not damage the paper, even if you press down firmly.

Turn over for more instructions ▶▶

4. Apply glue to the long, narrow tab and fold the whole segment to make a point. There will be a narrow folded tab at the front and back on the base of the point.

5. Cut out and fold the start/end segments as described in steps 1–3. Place two pieces of paper over each other and secure the photocopied template on top with paper clips. These two identical points have an additional tab each.

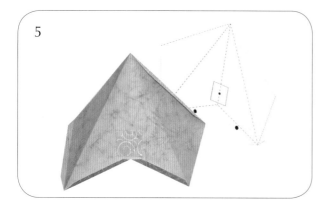

The start/end segments also have holes marked on them for tying the star together once finished. Glue a small square of paper behind the holes for added stability.

6. Poke a hole through each segment with a paper pricking tool or thumbtack and pull the thread halfway through.

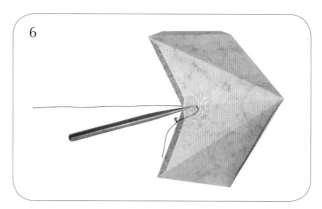

Fold up the two tabs marked with a bold black dot and glue to the inside of the point to reinforce it. Tie a small wooden bead to one end of the thread to stop it slipping.

7. Apply glue to the long tab and glue the point together. At the base of the point there should still be a visible tab.

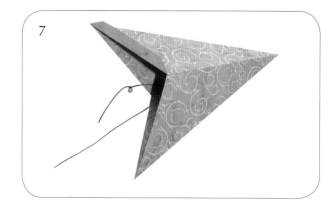

8. Now glue a middle segment to the start/end segment. Apply glue to the folded tabs on both (marked orange here). Turn the right segment over so that the grey glue strip is facing down, then press both segments together. If you carefully open them up, you can see that the tabs are still visible on the outside of the star.

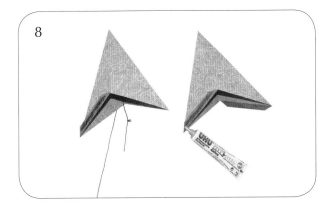

9. Hold the segments exactly over each other with pegs.

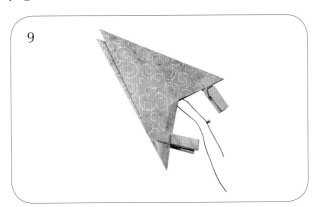

10. Join them all together in this way.

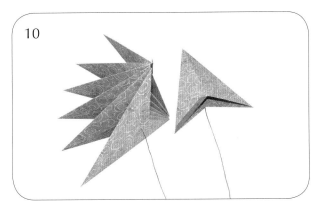

11. To open up the star, knot both threads together. This is easiest to accomplish when the star is hanging and if there is an extra person available to help. When the star is not hanging, the top opens up a little, but the weight of the star closes the gap when hanging.

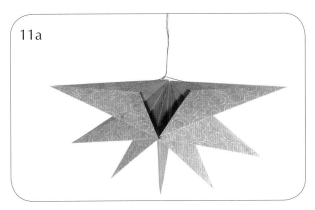

First frost

In blue and silver shards

Star size: 30 cm (12 in)

You will need

- ◊ 12 sheets of blue paper, 15 x 15 cm (6 x 6 in)
- ◊ 12 sheets of silver paper, 15 x 15 cm (6 x 6 in)

Template

- ◊ See page 151

1. Fold twelve blue and twelve silver segments, as described on pages 86–88. Place the template over these segments, outline with a pencil and cut out.
2. Apply a line of glue (where indicated in grey) to one of the blue segments and press a silver segment against it. Repeat this process for the remaining ten segments, alternating blue and silver. Unfold the star and glue the start and end points together.

Tip
You can make this star with a single colour or make your own wonderful combinations with as many colours as you like.

The big bang

In glowing colours

You will need

◊ 11 or 12 sheets of colour-blended paper, 15 x 15 cm (6 x 6 in)
◊ Red cotton thread, 30 cm (12 in)

Tip

Experiment with the size of the gap you leave when tying your knot. If the star won't unfold, cut the thread and pull a new thread through.

Templates

◊ See page 151

1. Fold and glue all segments up to step 8 as shown on pages 86 – 88. Arrange all the segments so that their colours blend in the same direction.
2. Place the template over your folded segments – the end with the holes should be the red end of your segments. Mark both holes with a pencil and punch them through. Repeat this process for the remaining ten or eleven segments and cut them out.
3. Glue along the indicated grey line of each segment and attach it to an adjacent segment, always making sure that the holes are exactly aligned.
4. Pull the thread through one row of holes and then back through the other row of holes. When you tie the thread, leave a two-finger gap between star and knot.
5. Unfold the star, add a final line of glue to the end segment and glue it to the first one.

Christmas star

In dark red

You will need

◊ 6 sheets of red paper, A4 (US letter)
◊ 2 wooden beads
◊ Red cotton thread, 120 cm (48 in) long

Template

◊ See page 152

1. Following the instructions for the closed Messina star on pages 89–91, place two sheets of paper over each other with your desired colour or pattern face down. Attach the template for the middle segment with four paper clips.
2. Cut out the small stars with a craft knife and cutting mat, then cut around the outlines with a craft knife and ruler. Detach the template and use it as a reference to score and fold the dashed lines on your segments. Repeat with a second photocopy of the middle template and two more sheets of paper so you can produce two more middle segments.
3. Apply glue to the long tabs and glue all four middle segments together.
4. Now attach the photocopy of the start/end template to two more sheets of your chosen paper. Cut out and fold the segments as before, allowing for the extra tab.
5. Cut an additional two paper squares of 2.5 x 2.5 cm (1 x 1 in). Fold these in half and glue onto each start/end segment where the rectangle is marked on the template – these won't show when the star is finished as they will be on the inside of the segments.

6. Prick a hole through the centre of each rectangle and pull through a 60 cm (24 in) thread. Attach a small wooden bead to the ends of both threads, then glue each segment to its adjacent middle segment. Unfold the star and knot both threaded ends together.

Tip
Remember the template shows dashed lines for valley folds and dot-dashed lines for mountain folds.

Drifting snowflakes

In sparkling white

You will need

◊ 5 sheets of white, waterproof paper, 20 x 20 cm (8 x 8 in)

Template

◊ See page 153

1. First, fold five segments following the instructions up to step 8 for the open Messina star on pages 86–88. Now fold the segment exactly in half along the dashed line and unfold. Apply glue to the area marked in grey and fold again.
2. Following the diagrams on page 153, place each template over the folded segment, outline and cut out the segment shape (c).
3. Apply a line of glue where indicated in grey (d), place a new segment exactly over the first and secure in place. Repeat for the remaining three points, unfold the star, glue the ends together and decorate festively.

White and gold star

A tasteful combination

Star size: 40 cm (16 in)

You will need

◊ 12 or 14 sheets of white patterned paper,
20 x 20 cm (8 x 8 in)
◊ White string, 30 cm (12 in)

Template

◊ See page 153

1. Fold and glue the sheets of paper up to step 8 of the instructions for the open Messina star on pages 86–88.
2. Place the template over the folded segment, punch the holes at the base, then cut out the point. Repeat this process until you have made twelve or fourteen segments. (If the star is too taut when unfolded, more than twelve will be needed.)
3. Apply a line of glue to the grey marked centre of one of the segments, then attach it to its adjacent segment, making sure the punched holes are aligned. Glue the remaining segments in the same way.
4. Thread the string through one row of holes and back through the other. Remember to leave a space before you tie a knot or you will not be able to unfold the star properly. Unfold the star, apply a line of glue to the last segment and glue it to the first.

Lilac snowflakes

Beautiful and calming

Star size: 19 cm (7 ½ in)

You will need

- ◊ 7 sheets of purple patterned paper, 20 x 20 cm (8 x 8 in)
- ◊ Purple wooden beads
- ◊ Purple string, 120 cm (48 in)

Template

- ◊ See page 154

1. Place three sheets of paper with your desired pattern face down. Then attach your copy of the middle segment template.
2. Cut along the solid lines with a craft knife and ruler on a cutting mat, remove the template, and score the dashed lines with a ruler and empty ballpoint pen.
3. Fold along the scored lines according to their markings: dashed lines for valley folds and dot-dashed lines for mountain folds. Repeat with a second photocopy and two more sheets of paper so that you have five middle segments.
4. Apply glue to the long narrow tabs and construct the segments into points according to the instructions for the closed Messina star on pages 89–91.
5. Attach a photocopy of the start/end segment template to your final two sheets of paper. Cut out the shapes, score and fold.
6. Cut out two additional paper squares, 2.5 x 2.5 cm (1 x 1 in), fold in half and glue at the marked rectangles. Prick through the centre of each segment's square and pull through a 60 cm (24 in) length of string. Knot a wooden bead to the end of each thread to hold it in place.
7. To finish, glue all segments together, unfold the star and tie both strings to each other.

Midnight blue star

With star patterns

Star size: 19 cm (7 ½ in)

You will need

◊ 7 sheets of blue and white patterned paper,
  20 x 20 cm (8 x 8 in)
◊ 2 blue wooden beads
◊ Blue string, 120 cm (48 in)

Template

◊ See pages 155–156

1. Place three sheets of paper over each other, patterned side down, with a copy of the middle segment template securely fixed on.
2. First cut out the stars using a craft knife and cutting mat, then cut around the edges of the template. Remove the cut-out photocopy and score the dashed and dot-dashed lines with a ruler and an empty ballpoint pen. Repeat this process with a second photocopy and two more sheets to make five middle segments.
3. Apply glue to the long narrow tab and construct them into points as on pages 89–91.
4. Secure a photocopy of the start/end segment template to your final two pieces of paper. Cut out the segments, score and fold as above.
5. Cut out two paper squares, 2.5 x 2.5 cm (1 x 1 in), fold in half and glue to the inside of both start/end segments at the marked rectangle. Prick through both squares and pull 60 cm (24 in) of string through each of them. Knot a wooden bead to the end of each thread to secure them in place.
6. Glue each start/end segment into a point, attach to the other segments, unfold the star and tie the strings together to hold everything in place.

Solar flares

In three variations

Star size: 15–30 cm (6–12 in)

- •

You will need

Large star
◊ 7 sheets of red paper, 15 x 15 cm (6 x 6 in)
◊ 7 sheets of gold paper, 15 x 15 cm (6 x 6 in)

Small star
◊ 3 sheets of red paper, 15 x 15 cm (6 x 6 in)
◊ 3 sheets of gold paper, 15 x 15 cm (6 x 6 in)

Star with long and short points
◊ 6 sheets of red paper, 15 x 15 cm (6 x 6 in)
◊ 6 sheets of gold paper, 15 x 15 cm (6 x 6 in)

- •

Templates

◊ See pages 156–157

Large star

1. Make fourteen pointed segments using all the sheets of paper and the large template.
2. Fold and glue the star together using the instructions for the open Messina star on pages 86–88.
3. For a variation on this star, alternate red and gold segments.

Small star

1. Fold three red and three gold segments up to step 8 of the open Messina star instructions on pages 86–88.
2. Fold the segments exactly in half along the dashed line shown on the template, unfold and apply a line of glue. Fold in half again (3a and 3b, page 157).
3. Place template 3 over the folded point, outline and cut out the segment point (3c, page 157).
4. Apply a line of glue to the segment as shown in step 11 of the open Messina star instructions, page 87), then attach to a different coloured segment. Continue gluing the remaining segments together, alternating the colours as you go. Unfold the star and glue the ends together.

Star with long and short points

1. Fold six red and six gold segments following the instructions up to step 8 (pages 86–87).
2. Place template 2 over the red segments, outline and cut out the points.
3. Fold the gold segments in half, unfold again, apply a line of glue and stick down in half again (3a and 3b, page 157).
4. Place template 3 over the gold segments, outline and cut out (3c).
5. Apply a line of glue to a finished gold segment (step 11, page 87), then attach to a red segment. Glue the remaining ten points in place this way, alternating the colours. Unfold the star and glue the ends together.

Luminous gold star

With lantern-paper windows

Star size: 42 cm (16 ½ in)

You will need

- ◊ 7 sheets of thick gold card, A4 (US letter)
- ◊ 4 sheets of white lantern paper, A4 (US letter)
- ◊ 2 yellow wooden beads
- ◊ Yellow or gold string, 120 cm (48 in)

Template

- ◊ See page 157

Tip

You will need thick card stock to make a stable frame for this star as it has lantern paper glued to the back.

1. Cut out, score and fold two start/end segments and five middle segments using the instructions for the closed Messina star on pages 89–91.
2. Glue a photocopy of the lantern paper shape on page 157 to a piece of card and cut out. Use this template to produce fourteen windows from your lantern paper, i.e. two pieces per segment.
3. Glue the lantern window pieces to the insides of your seven segments.
4. Prick holes in the start/end segments where indicated and pull through 60 cm of string. Knot a wooden bead to each one and place it on the inside of the segment.

5. Fold back and glue the tabs marked with a black dot to stabilise the edges when opening and shutting the star.
6. Apply glue to the long tabs on each segment and fold to construct each point.
7. Carefully glue some small stars in place on the lantern paper. You can cut your own from gold card or use stickers. (tweezers are useful for the fiddly bits!)
8. Now glue all the middle segments together, holding the tabs firmly inside the adjacent point each time.
9. Finally, glue the start/end segments to each end of the chain. Now you can unfold the star and hang it up.

Solino Stars

Solino stars: the basics

Paper

Any paper that can be folded precisely is suitable for these stars. We recommend parchment paper, but anything between 90 and 110 gsm (60 and 80 lb) should do. The paper will need to be long enough to trim down to 5 x 35 cm (2 x 14 in) to make a star roughly 10 cm (4 in) in diameter.

Drawing the guidelines

Each Solino project's pencil guidelines involve very precise, small measurements. As a result, they are given in millimetres rather than inches, so you will need a metric ruler.

1. Lay your paper strip horizontally on a cutting mat.
2. Use a pencil and ruler to mark the measurements given in the star project instructions, first along the right edge, then bend the paper across to mark matching lines on left edge.
3. Very lightly score the horizontal lines between these marks with a blunt needle and ruler. Take care not to damage the paper or foil with the needle.

4. Draw an additional vertical line on the far right side of the paper 5 mm (¼ in) wide. This will be the gluing tab to join the ends together after the star has been cut.

Folding the strips

Take your time to fold as exactly as possible for a good result:

1. Fold back (mountain fold) the right tab, 5 mm wide.
2. Turn the strip over. The guidelines should now be facing down and the gluing tab will be folded up on the right.
3. Valley fold in half (treat the edge of the tab as the end of the segment) and unfold.
4. Valley fold both ends in to meet the centre fold line, then unfold again. The strip will now be divided into four parts.
5. Start folding the accordion folds. Starting at the right end, valley fold inwards to the first fold line, then unfold.
6. Bend the first quarter fold line upwards (so it becomes a mountain fold), then bring it to the centre line and press down. Unfold.
7. Continue this pattern along the strip: fold the centre line up to a mountain fold and bring over to the third quarter line and press down. Unfold.
8. Fold the third quarter line to the end of the strip. Now your strip will be divided into eight with an accordion fold (four mountain folds, four valley folds).
9. Repeat this process twice more to make an accordion fold with sixteen mountain folds. Even longer strips will need more folds, as you will see in the individual projects.

Tip

Make sure the side with the guidelines is always facing down when folding.

Cutting the points

Once you have finished folding you can start cutting the star's pattern out. To do this, hold the folded strip with the tab facing up towards the right. Now, starting from the bottom right, begin cutting the segment one pleat at a time, according to the guidelines for each project.

Continue cutting the points pleat for pleat until the whole strip is completed.

Cutting the pattern

Rotate the strip 90° and hold it so the points are facing right. Again, cut pleat for pleat following the individual guidelines.

Forming the star

1. When you have finished cutting the strip, unfold the gluing tab, apply a little glue and stick to the start so the strip forms a circle.
2. Once the glue is dry, use a needle and thread to sew through the base of each pleat.
3. Once the needle has passed through each pleat, pull the thread and fan the circle flat. Bring the edges all neatly together in the centre and knot the thread carefully.

Hanging the star

Thread a needle and pull it through the centre of one of the star's points.

Hang the star with the gluing tab facing downwards so it is less noticeable.

Designing your own templates

Cut a strip out of lightweight paper in your desired star size. Fold as described above, mark some guidelines and simply start cutting out different designs. Experiment until you are happy with the results. Transfer the template to the strip of your chosen paper.

Geometric stars

Tantalising in red

Star size: 7 cm (2 ¾ in)

··
· **You will need**
·
· ◊ Red parchment paper, 3.5 x 25 cm
·   (1 ³/₈ x 10 in)
··

Design

◊ 16 pleats with 4 or 8 guidelines

To make these stars, see the basic instructions for folding and cutting Solino stars on pages 112–113. Mark the guidelines and cut out the strip pleat for pleat using the instructions and the designs shown below.

Top star

Mark the guidelines at 5, 10, 13 and 17 mm.

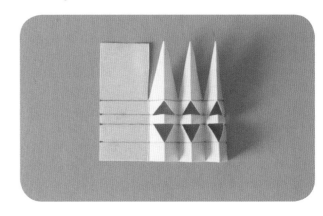

Bottom star

Mark the guidelines at 6, 15, 17, 21, 23, 27, 29 and 32 mm.

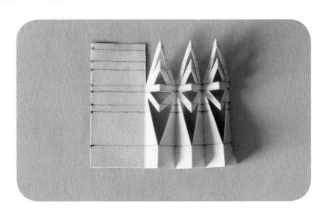

Blue variations

A beautiful hanging trio

You will need

◊ Blue parchment paper, 5 x 35 cm (2 x 14 in)

Design

◊ 16 pleats each. See the basic instructions on pages 112–113.

Left star

1. For this star, mark the guidelines at 7, 14, 17, 24, 27 and 37 mm.
2. Cut the point of this star to the second guideline as shown in the photo. The first guideline is for a later decoration.

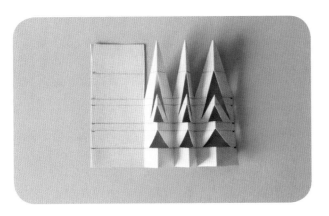

Bottom star

Mark the guidelines at 5, 19, 21, 26, 28, 34, 36, 41, 43 and 47 mm.

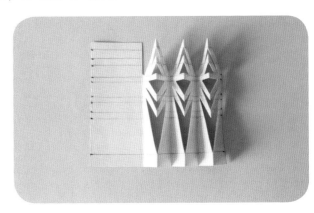

Top star

Mark the guidelines at 7, 12, 14, 17, 19, 21, 24, 27, 29, 34, 36, 38, 41 and 45 mm.

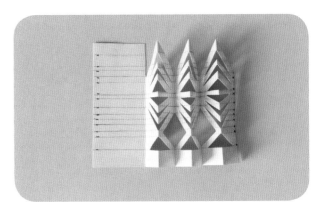

Intricate stars

Complex one- or two-sided patterns

You will need

◊ Blue parchment paper, 8.5 x 50 cm
(3 ⅝ x 20 in)

Design

◊ 32 pleats. See the basic instructions on
pages 112–113.

1. Mark the guidelines at 10, 25, 28, 35, 38, 44, 48,
58, 62 and 73 mm.
2. You can make two stars using this template. For
the star on the right, cut the pleats on the front
side only. For the star on the left, cut an extra hole
in the pleats from the underside too.

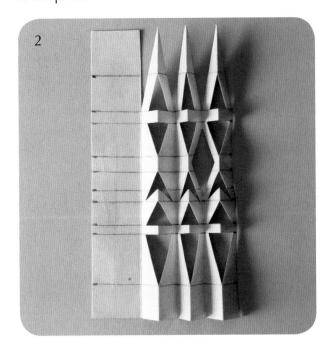

Elegant snowflake

Delicate and striking

You will need

◊ White or cream parchment paper,
  15.5 x 70 cm (6 x 27 ½ in)

Design

◊ 32 pleats. Follow the basic instructions on
  pages 112 – 113.

1. Mark the guidelines at 20, 25, 30, 35, 39, 44, 48,
   54, 57, 66 and 81 mm.

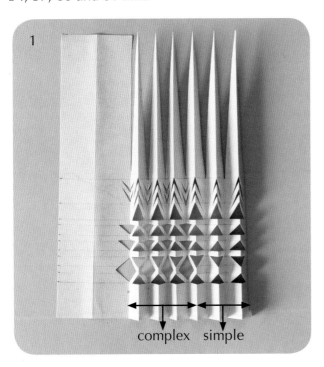

complex   simple

2. The completed star in the photo shows the simpler
   of the two design options given in the guideline
   photo. Add in the extra underside cuts for an
   added challenge.

Hypernova

For expert star makers

Star size: 50 cm (20 in)

- -

You will need

◊ Red parchment paper, 25 x 140 cm
  (10 x 55 in)

- -

Design

An enormous accordion fold with 64 pleats. See the basic instructions on pages 112–113 for how to fold and cut out the star pleat by pleat.

1. Glue two strips of paper together if necessary to achieve the desired length. Use a bone folder for crisp pleats! You will also need silence and perseverance to complete this star.

2. Mark the guidelines at 25, 31, 35, 40, 43, 48, 55, 60, 69, 71, 74, 76, 79, 81, 84, 87, 97, 99, 102, 104, 109, 111, 117, 119, 122, 125, 127, 131, 136, 138, 142 and 146 mm.

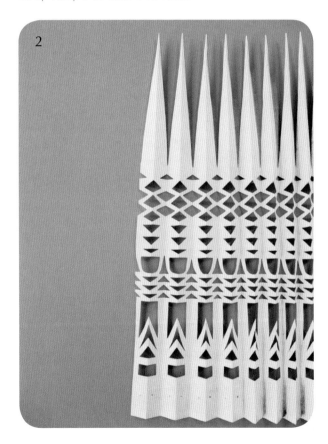

Venezia Stars

Venezia stars: the basics

Paper

Very thick paper upwards of 110 gsm (75 lb) is perfect for Venezia stars.

How to make the template

Photocopy your chosen template (this example uses the Star crystal template on page 158) and glue to a piece of thick card. Cut the template out as precisely as possible using a craft knife, cutting mat and metal ruler.

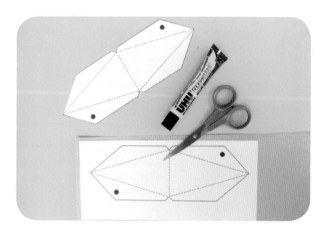

Making the star segments

1. Place the template on your chosen paper, outline with a pencil and cut out. Or, if you are experienced with a craft knife, you can cut straight around the template edge.
2. Place the metal ruler where the folding lines are indicated and score very gently using a craft knife. The dashed lines show valley folds; to score dot-dashed lines, which are mountain folds, turn the template over and score on the underside.

Tip

Experiment with leftover pieces of card to discover the best pressure needed for scoring without cutting right through the paper.

3. Apply glue or double-sided tape to the tabs marked with black dots. These strips are slightly larger than their corresponding tabs, so that when the segments are assembled, the edges can be securely tucked inside the point.

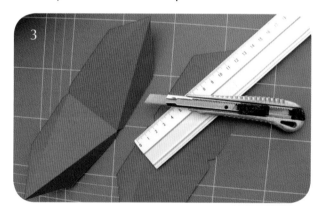

Making the lantern windows

1. Use the templates provided to cut out your window shapes with a craft knife.
2. Cut slightly larger, corresponding shapes from lantern paper and glue on the inside of the segment.

Small Venezia star with eight points

Each eight-pointed star is made out of twelve segments. In the step-by-step instructions, double-sided tape is used, but you can use all-purpose glue if you prefer. Either way, make sure you glue or tape the larger tab marked with a black dot.

1. Glue two segments together as shown (1a), add the third segment (1b) and turn the whole piece over (1c).

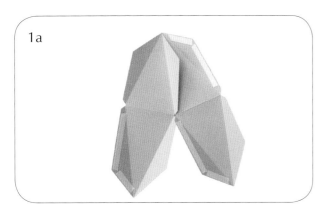

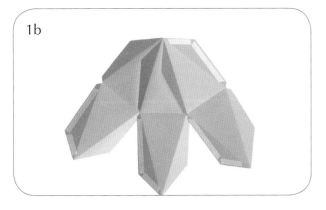

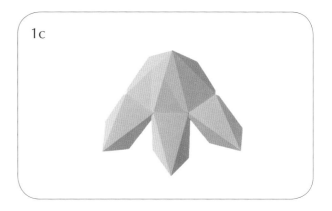

2. Glue the segments to make a point.

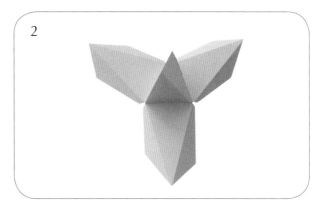

3. Glue the fourth (3a) and then the fifth (3b) segments to the left side of the lower segment. Then join them to each other to complete the second point (3c).

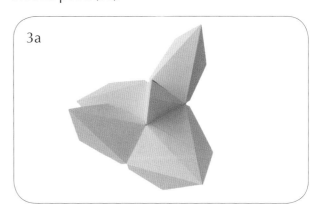

Turn over for more instructions ▶▶

127

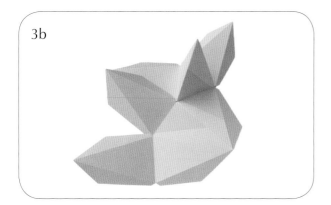

3b

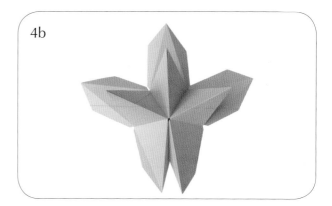

4b

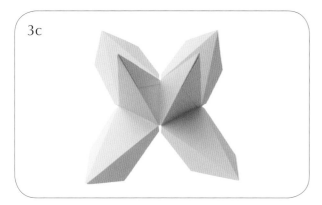

3c

5. Glue the two points at the bottom together (5a). Glue the eighth segment to the left side of them, then make them into the fourth point (5b).

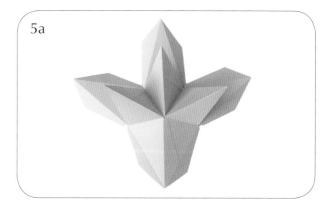

5a

4. Glue the sixth segment to the left side of the bottom right point (4a). Attach the seventh segment to the sixth and then glue them together to make the third point (4b).

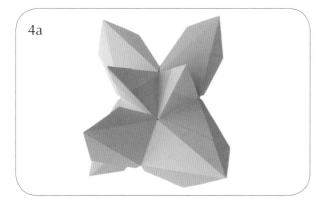

4a

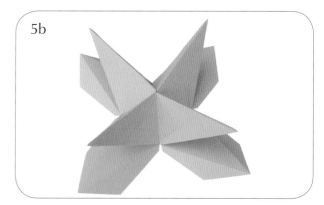

5b

6. Turn the whole piece over (6a). Glue the ninth segment horizontally between both lower points (6b). Repeat this process between the points of the right and left sides (6c).

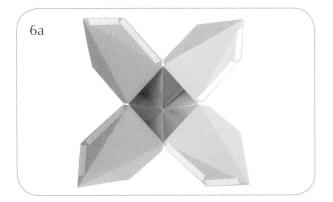

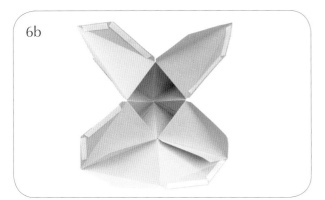

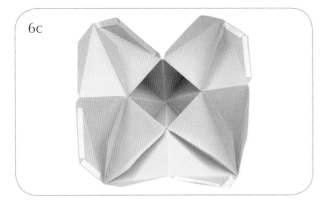

7. Glue the bottom right segments together to make the fifth point.

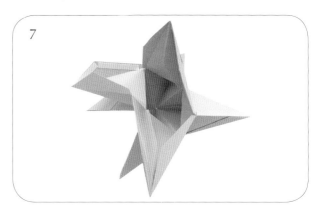

8. Glue the bottom left segments together to make the sixth point.

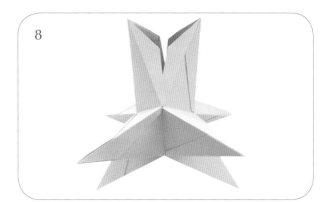

Turn over for more instructions ▶▶

Hanging a small Venezia star

9. Add the last segment horizontally between the two top points. To do this, glue the last segment to the front left side (9a). Fold the segment between the two top points and glue the seventh point together (9b). Finally, close and glue the eighth point together (9c). Don't forget to attach a hanging string if you want to suspend the star.

The small and large Venezia stars are hung in different ways.

To hang up a small star, tie a small wooden bead to some string and place the beaded end into the final point of your star before gluing it together.

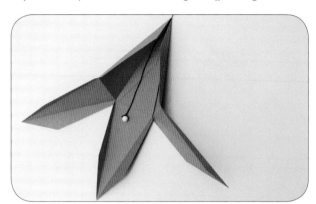

9a

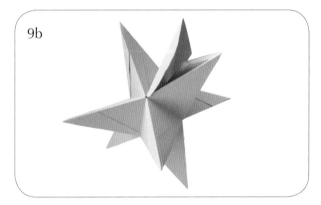

9b

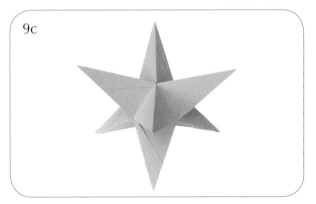

9c

Large Venezia star with twenty points

Each large twenty-pointed star is made out of thirty segments. This example has yellow and red segments to help make the instructions clearer.

1. Glue the first three segments together into a point as you would for the small Venezia star.

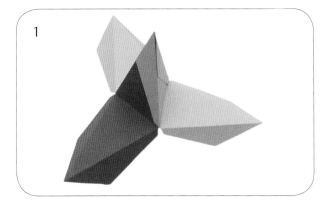

2. Make a second point identical to the first and place both points beside each other (2a). Glue the top two segments to each other to connect these points. This makes both the lower segments cross over each other (2b).

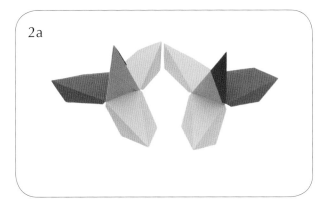

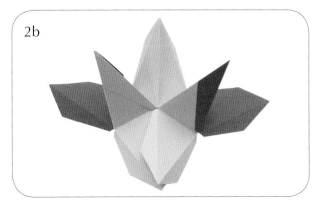

3. Glue a segment horizontally between the two bottom segments (3a and 3b).

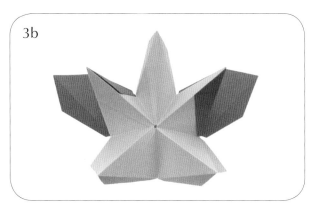

4. Glue a red segment to the lower right side of this new horizontal segment as shown (4a). Wrap the segment round to the right and glue to form the third point (4b).

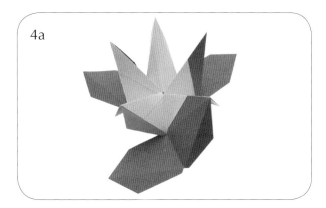

Turn over for more instructions ▶▶

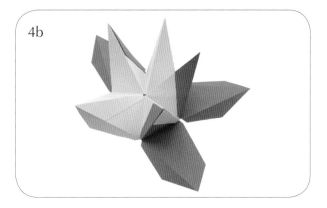

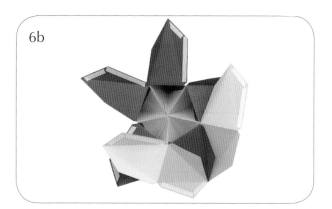

5. Make the fourth and fifth points by adding new red segments to the remaining yellow segments and securing them in the same way.

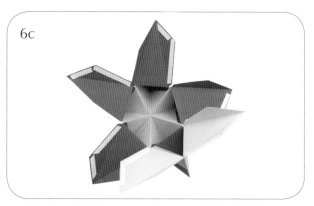

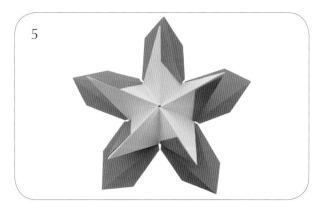

6. Turn the whole shape over. Glue a yellow segment onto the bottom left side of the lower right segment (6a). Glue another yellow segment on the other side of the same red segment (6b). Wrap these yellow segments round and glue in place to make the sixth point (6c).

7. Glue two yellow segments to each of the remaining four red segments and make into points in the same way. This should form a five-pointed star shape in the centre with five pairs of yellow segments fanning out from it (7a). These ten yellow segments are held back in figure 7b with pegs to give you a better view.

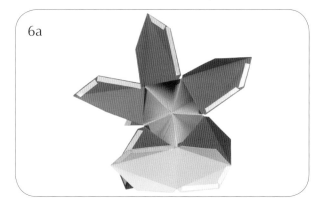

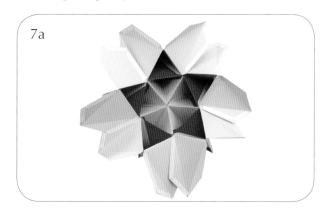

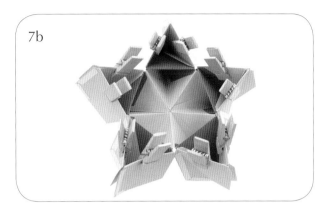

7b

8. Remove the pegs from the two bottom yellow segments. Join them together (8a) and repeat this process four times with the other yellow segments. You will now have five yellow open points (8b).

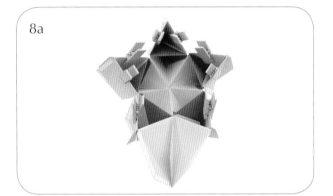

8a

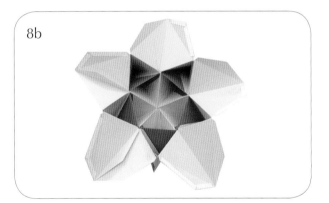

8b

9. Glue a red segment to the upper edge of the top right point (9a). Wrap the red segment over to make the eleventh point (9b). Fold back the red flap left over (9c).

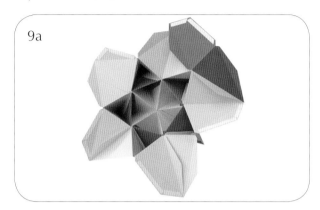

9a

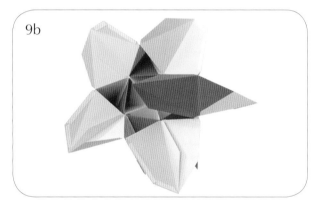

9b

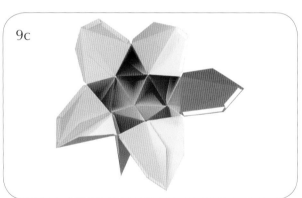

9c

10. Repeat this step with the remaining four points around the star. In figure 10 the red points are pegged back to give you a better overview.

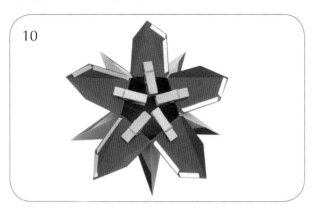

10

11. Remove the pegs from the top two segments, then glue a new yellow segment horizontally between them (11a and 11b). Remove the peg to the left of these joined segments and glue another yellow segment to join the two together (11c). Close up and join the two new yellow segments to make the sixteenth point (11d).

11a

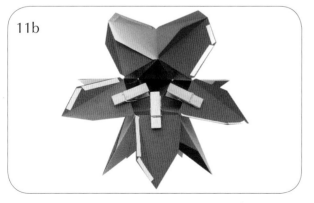

11b

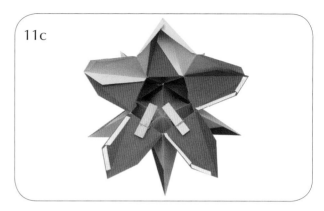

11c

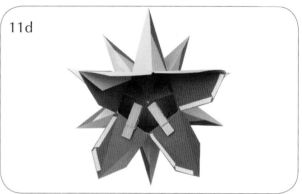

11d

12. Remove the next peg and add another yellow segment to join two red segments as before (12a). Join it to the previous yellow segment to form the seventeenth point (12b). Repeat for the penultimate segment (12c) and construct the eighteenth point (12d). Insert the last segment into the gap to make the last two points. Glue the segment to the right side, then fold it into the gap and glue in place (12e – g).

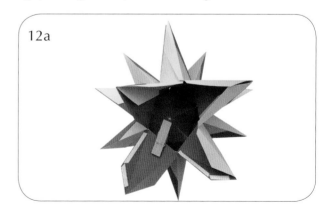

12a

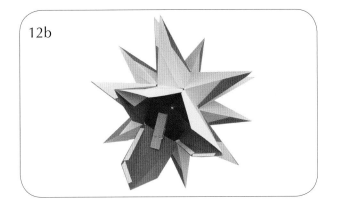

12b

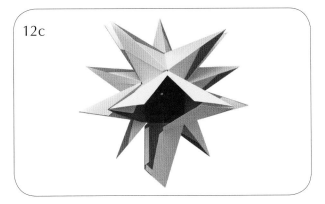

12c

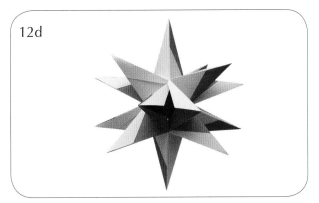

12d

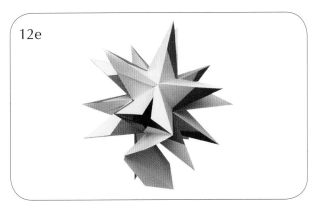

12e

12f

12g

Hanging a twenty-pointed Venezia star

To hang a large star, tie some string to half a matchstick or a toothpick. Push the stick into the largest hole between a set of five points. When you pull on the thread, the wood will lie horizontally inside the star.

Star crystal

With subtle snowflakes

You will need

◊ 12 sheets of white textured paper,
  A4 (US letter)
◊ Snowflake punch, diameter 1.2 cm (½ in)

Template

◊ See page 158

1. Make twelve segments using either of the provided templates.
2. Punch out the snowflake shapes, making sure they will not be covered by the gluing flaps of adjacent points when the star is assembled.
3. Follow the instructions for the small Venezia star on pages 127–130 to assemble the star.

Exotic stars

With beaded tassels

Star size: 35 cm (14 in)

You will need

◊ 12 sheets of black glitter paper, A4 (US letter)
◊ Assorted purple, amber and glass-imitation beads
◊ Transparent hanging string

Tip
Cutting glitter paper will quickly blunt a craft knife, so make sure you break off the tip regularly to avoid damaging the paper.

Template

◊ See page 158

1. Make twelve segments from your chosen paper using either of the templates provided.
2. Construct your star using the basic instructions for a small eight-pointed Venezia star on pages 127–130.
3. Before closing your top and bottom points, add an invisible hanging string to the top, then add a beautiful trail of beads from the bottom – it will look as if it is floating away…

Large white stars

In a morning sky

Star size: 41 cm (16 in)

```
You will need

◊ 30 sheets of cream-coloured patterned
   paper, A4 (US letter)
```

Template

◊ See page 158

1. Use either of the templates provided to make thirty segments.
2. See the instructions for the large, twenty-pointed Venezia star on pages 131–135 for gluing the segments together.

```
                    Tip
You can make a shorter version of this star by
designing your own smaller segments. Shorter
and blunter points are easier to glue together.
```

Shining beacon
To welcome you home

Star size: 41 cm (16 in)

3

You will need

◊ 30 sheets of thick red card, A4 (US letter)
◊ 15 sheets of orange lantern paper, A4
◊ Fairy lights

Templates

◊ See page 159

1. To make the thirty segments, each with their triangular window space, use either of the templates provided.
2. Each segment has two windows, but one segment will be left without lantern paper. So cut out fifty-eight lantern-paper triangles using the template provided and glue them to the inside of each star segment.

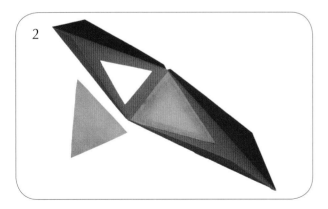

2

3. Following the instructions for the large Venezia star on pages 131–135, glue the star together point by point. In this photo the last segment – the one without lantern paper – has not yet been glued in place.

4. Insert your fairy lights through both of the openings in the last segment and glue the segment in place. Glue some extra card to the inside of the frame between the triangles to strengthen it.
5. Switch on the fairy lights and watch your star glow!

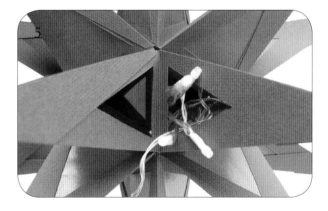

5

Templates

Filino templates

Stars within stars

Page 43
Enlarge to 200%

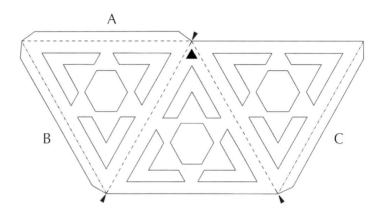

Star sphere

Page 44
Enlarge to 200%

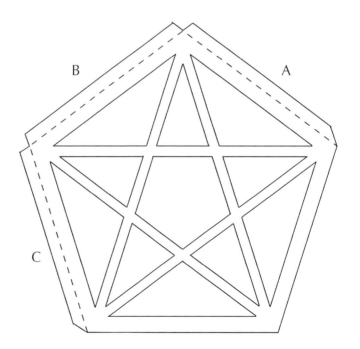

Three suns

Page 45
Enlarge to 200%

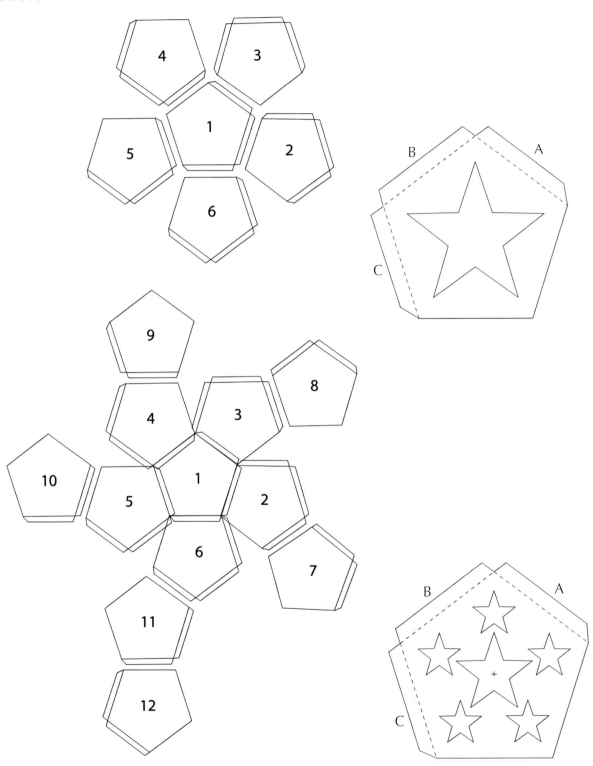

Ladder star

Page 47
Enlarge to 200%

Pendant

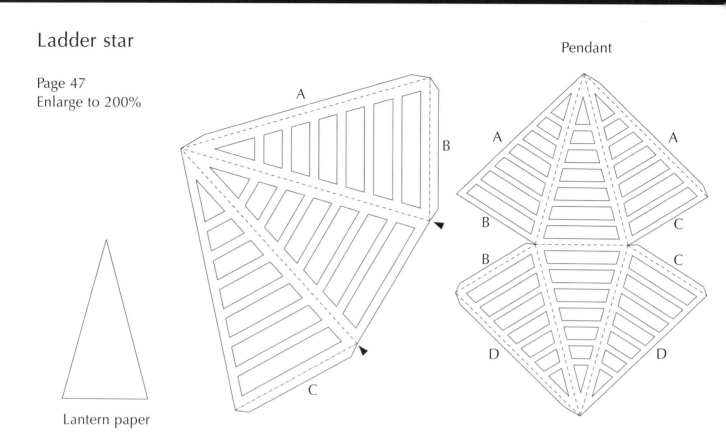

Lantern paper

· ·

Christmas trees

Page 49
Enlarge to 200%

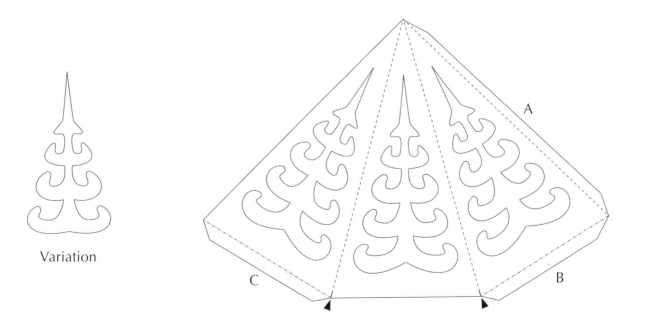

Variation

Steeple star

Page 51
Enlarge to 200%

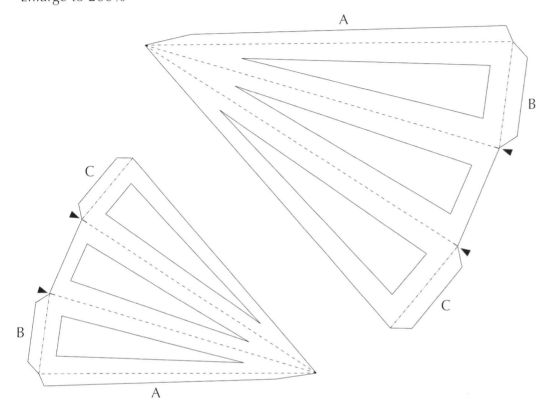

Love hearts

Page 53
Enlarge to 200%

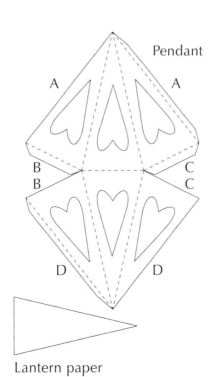

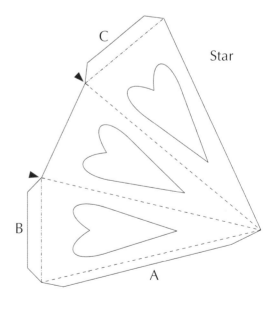

Froebel templates

Supernova

Page 71
Enlarge to 200%

2 x

Poinsettias

Page 73

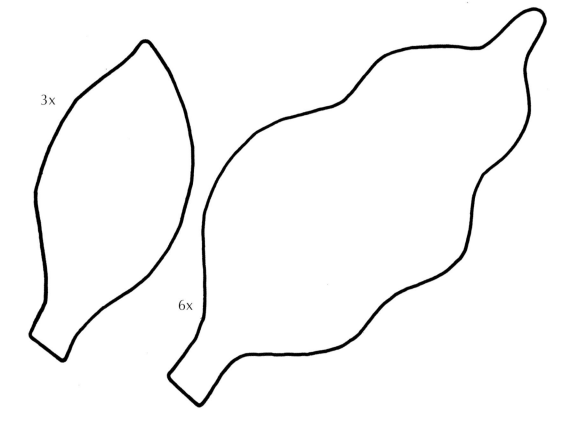

3x

6x

Messina templates

First frost

Page 93
3.6 cm (1 ³/₈ in)

3.6 cm (1 ³/₈ in)

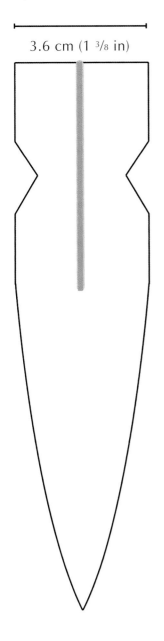

The big bang

Page 95
4.7 cm (1 ³/₄ in)

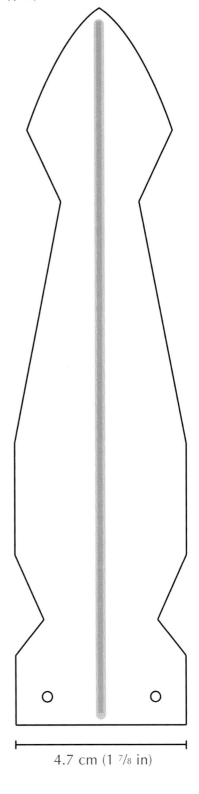

4.7 cm (1 ⁷/₈ in)

Christmas star

Page 97
Enlarge to 200%

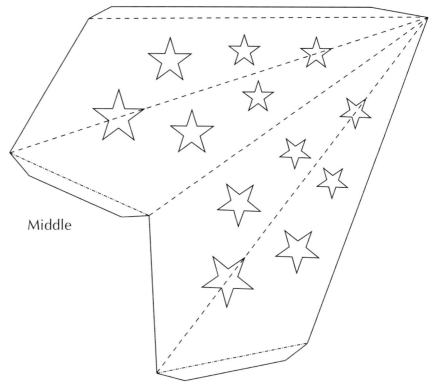

Middle

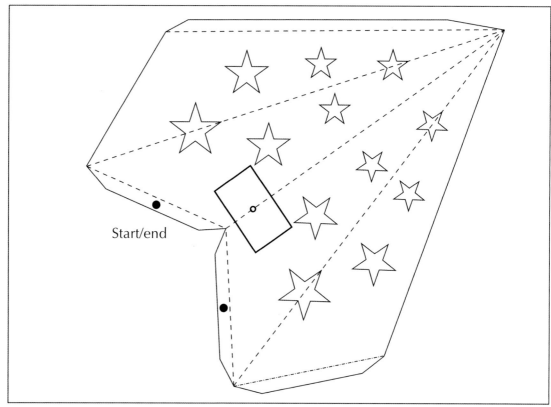

Start/end

Drifting snowflakes

Page 99
Enlarge to 200%
4.5 cm (1 ¾ in)

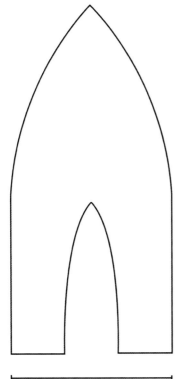

4.5 cm (1 ¾ in)

A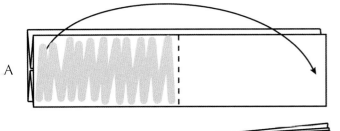

B

C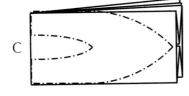

D

White and gold star

Page 101
4.5 cm (1 ¾ in)

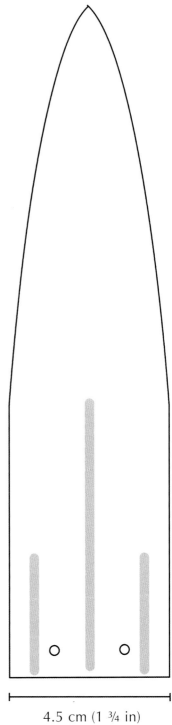

4.5 cm (1 ¾ in)

Lilac snowflakes

Page 103
Enlarge to 200%
For folding paper 20 x 20 cm (8 x 8 in)

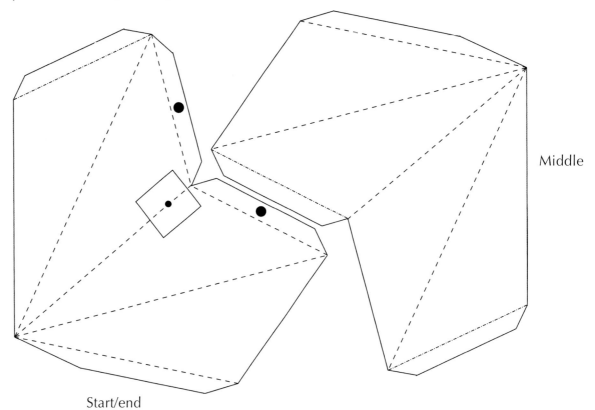

Middle

Start/end

Midnight blue star

Page 105
Enlarge to 200%
Blue star with cut out stars
Version for A4 paper (US letter)

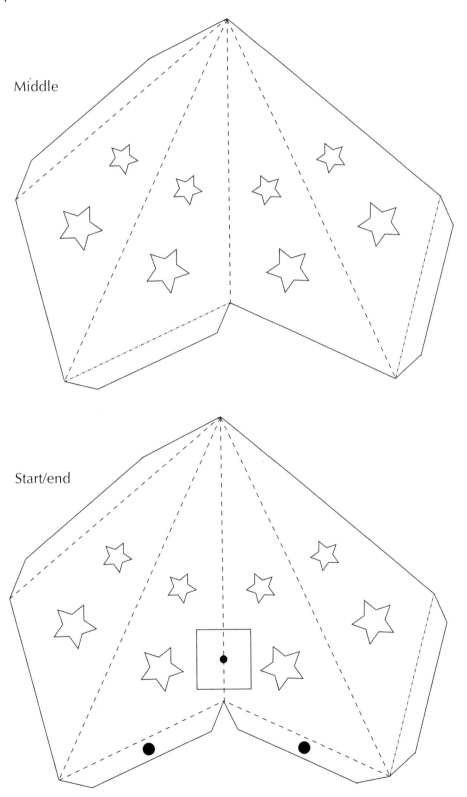

Middle

Start/end

Midnight blue star

Page 105
Enlarge to 200%
Version for 20 x 20 cm (8 x 8 in) folding paper

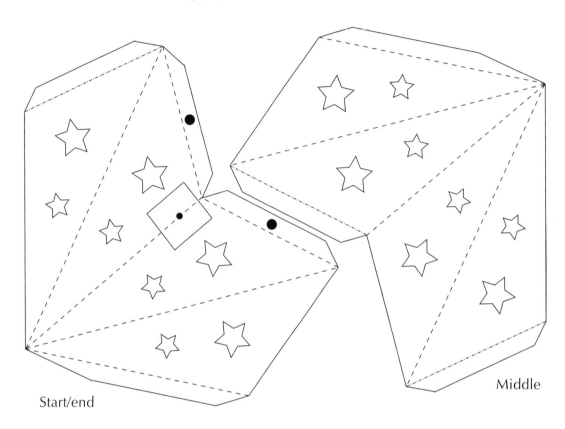

Start/end

Middle

Solar flares

Pages 106 – 107
Enlarge to 200%

Template 1: Large star
3.6 cm (1 ³/₈ in)

Template 2
3.6 cm (1 ³/₈ in)

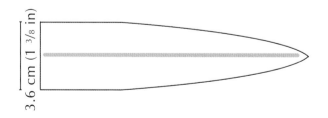

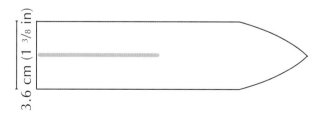

Template 3: Small star
Enlarge to 200%
3.6 cm (1 ³/₈ in)
Step by step instructions for small red-gold star

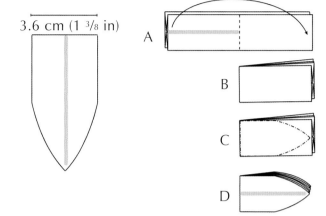

3.6 cm (1 ³/₈ in)

Luminous gold star

Page 109
Enlarge to 200%

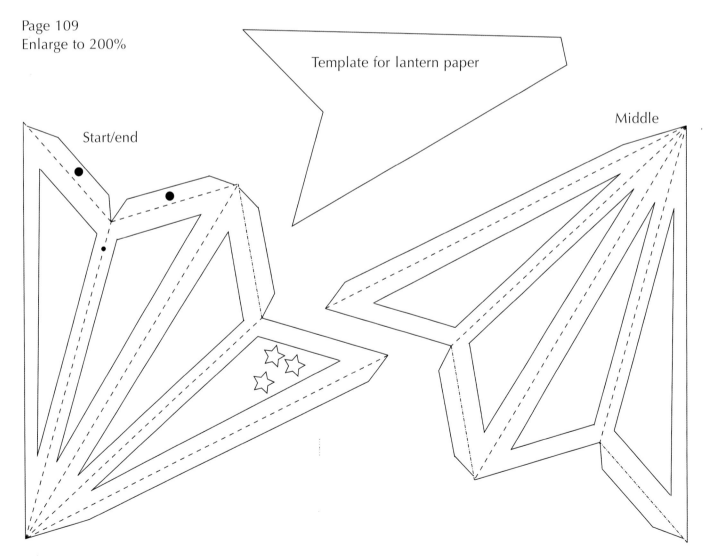

Template for lantern paper

Start/end

Middle

Venezia templates

Star crystal

Page 137
Enlarge to 200%
30 x 7 cm (12 x 2 ¾ in)

Exotic stars

Page 139
Enlarge to 200%

Large white stars

Page 141
Enlarge to 200%
29 x 7 cm (11 ½ x 2 ¾ in)

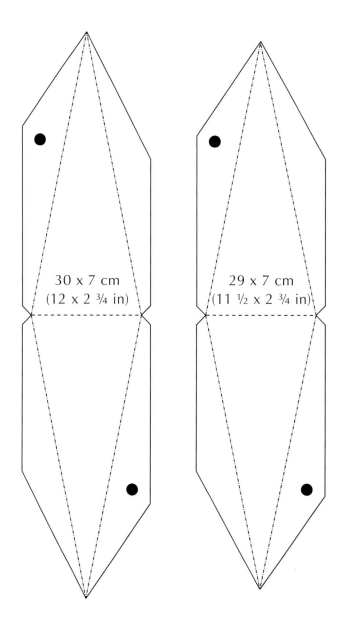

30 x 7 cm
(12 x 2 ¾ in)

29 x 7 cm
(11 ½ x 2 ¾ in)

Shining beacon

Page 143
Enlarge to 200%

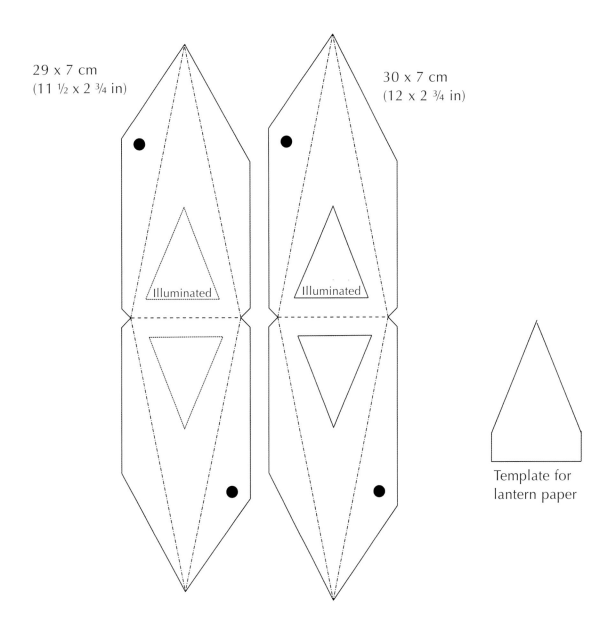

29 x 7 cm
(11 ½ x 2 ¾ in)

30 x 7 cm
(12 x 2 ¾ in)

Illuminated

Illuminated

Template for
lantern paper

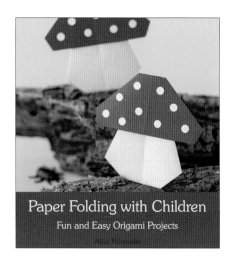

Paper Folding with Children
Fun and Easy Origami Projects
Alice Hörnecke

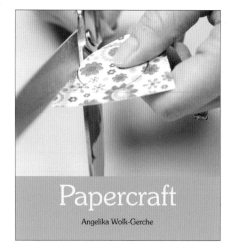

Papercraft
Angelika Wolk-Gerche

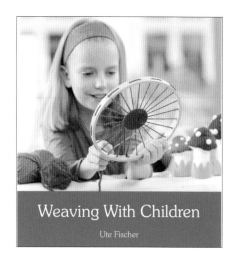

Weaving With Children
Ute Fischer

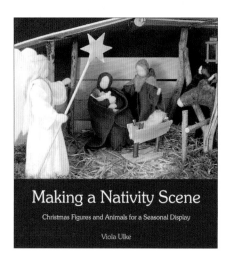

Making a Nativity Scene
Christmas Figures and Animals for a Seasonal Display
Viola Ulke

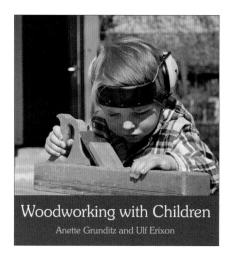

Woodworking with Children
Anette Grunditz and Ulf Erixon

Magical Window Stars
Frédérique Guéret

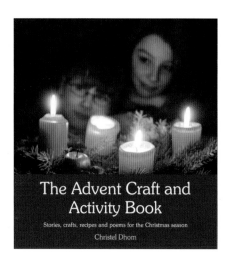

The Advent Craft and
Activity Book
Stories, crafts, recipes and poems for the Christmas season
Christel Dhom

Crafts Through the Year
Thomas and Petra Berger

The Christmas Craft Book
Thomas Berger